The
Sailing
Handbook

The Sailing Handbook

John Davies

Hamlyn
London·New York·Sydney·Toronto

Acknowledgements

Photographs

Beken of Cowes 8-9, 12, 21, 33, 34, 35, 82, 90-91, 107, 114-115, 128, 152, 186-187, 191, 195, 213; Hamlyn Group – David Johnson 27 top, 27 bottom, 30-31, 31 top right, 31 bottom, 36, 37, 50, 51 top, 51 centre, 51 bottom, 54, 57 top, 60, 72, 72-73, 80, 92, 94, 98 left, 98 right, 99, 100 left, 100 right, 101 top, 101 bottom left, 101 bottom right, 102 top, 102 bottom, 103 top, 103 bottom, 113, 117, 118, 121, 138, 140, 144, 151, 153 top, 153 bottom, 160, 172, 173, 174, 176-177, 180-181, 182, 190 top, 190 bottom, 192-193, 194, 209; Jane Herridge 75; Alan Hutchison Library 11, 22, 23, 106; Meteorological Office (M.O.) 165 centre left, M.O. – M. P. Garrod 164, M.O. – R. W. Mason 165 top left, M.O. – H. G. Mullett 165 bottom right, M.O. – Capt. T. Rigg 165 bottom left, M.O. – H. O. Robbins 165 centre right, M.O. – W. K. Young 165 top right; Overseas Containers Ltd 116; Barry Pickthall 2-3, 6-7, 57 bottom, 58, 64, 70-71, 81, 89, 93, 95, 211, 212; Science Museum, London 24; John Watney 13, 35 inset, 132, 154-155, 155, 210, 214, 215; John Watney – Jerry Young 208; Susan Watts 39; ZEFA – Bob Croxford 167.
Front jacket – main picture Barry Pickthall; inset Hamlyn Group – David Johnson. Back jacket – Barry Pickthall.

Illustrations

Peter Dennis; Bob Mathias.

Published 1981 by
The Hamlyn Publishing Group Limited
London · New York · Sydney · Toronto
Astronaut House, Feltham, Middlesex, England.

ISBN 0 600 36469 0

Printed in Italy

Contents

Introduction

All of us are likely to do better at anything if we have been properly taught, and this includes all kinds of sport, but the proper way of doing things is more important in sailing than in most other sports. If you do not do the right thing, in the right way and at the right time, when you are sailing, you can drown, or put at risk not only your own life but the lives of those who have to come to your rescue.

To use a sailing expression, the purpose of this book is to help you start off on the right tack. It is a simple, beginners' book, and you may already know some of what it has to tell you. Even if you do, it won't hurt to check that your knowledge is accurate.

Sailing is a wonderful leisure-time activity. You can take part in it at any age. You don't have to be athletic or particularly skilful physically. You can sail at all sorts of levels, from dodging about on some small lake to sailing round the world. You can race, or cruise, or just potter about.

Nowadays people sail on almost any bit of water deep enough to take a boat's keel: on rivers, lakes, reservoirs, even flooded gravel pits, to say nothing of the sea. Wherever you live, there is bound to be somewhere to sail

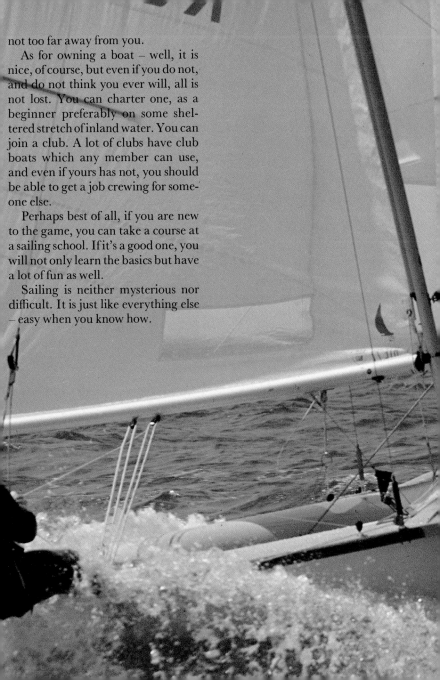

not too far away from you.

As for owning a boat – well, it is nice, of course, but even if you do not, and do not think you ever will, all is not lost. You can charter one, as a beginner preferably on some sheltered stretch of inland water. You can join a club. A lot of clubs have club boats which any member can use, and even if yours has not, you should be able to get a job crewing for someone else.

Perhaps best of all, if you are new to the game, you can take a course at a sailing school. If it's a good one, you will not only learn the basics but have a lot of fun as well.

Sailing is neither mysterious nor difficult. It is just like everything else – easy when you know how.

Using the Wind

The first thing to know about sailing is how a sailing vessel makes use of the wind.

The measure of such a vessel's efficiency is the extent to which she is able to move in one direction when the wind is trying to blow her in another.

The simplest effect of the wind on a sail may be illustrated by the movement of a leaf on the surface of a pond. It will be blown along in the same direction as the wind.

Square rig

The earliest seafarers under sail were blown along in this way. If the wind was blowing the way they wanted to go, they hoisted a sail. If it was not, they either had to wait for the wind to change, or had to resort to an even earlier method of propulsion – they had to row.

A square or oblong sail is the most effective for this kind of sailing, so this was the kind most of these early sailors chose. The top edge of the sail was attached to a *yard* (ie pole) hoisted up the mast to extend it, and the bottom corners were held out by ropes. To catch the wind the sail had to be hoisted at right-angles to it, that is, square across the vessel. As a result, this sail arrangement is known as square rig.

As ships became bigger, they ac-

quired more sails, with additional masts to hoist them on, until the days of the great windjammers arrived, with many sails and highly complicated rigging for supporting and con-

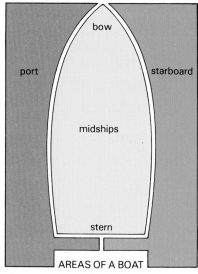

AREAS OF A BOAT

trolling them. In those days a sailor really did have to know the ropes! Centuries of experience and modification improved these vessels' sailing performance, but their square rig set a limit to the courses they could steer in relation to the wind. They could sail with the wind coming from behind or from the side, but they could not sail even diagonally into the wind, that is, the direction from which the wind is coming. Only fore-and-aft rigged vessels can do this.

The great days of sail! This square-rigger with a cloud of canvas is the Russian training ship Kruzenshtern.

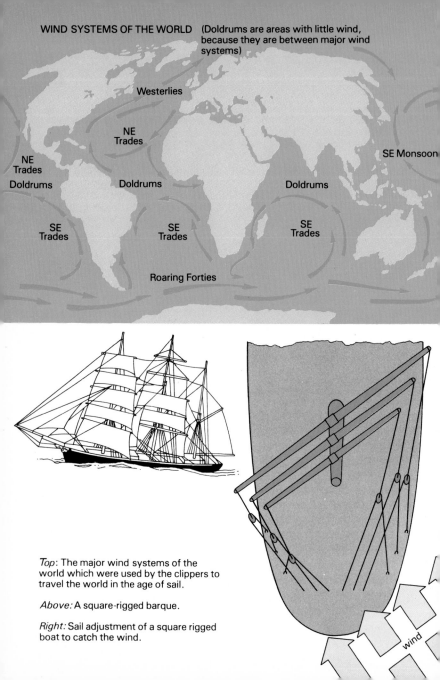

WIND SYSTEMS OF THE WORLD (Doldrums are areas with little wind, because they are between major wind systems)

Westerlies

NE Trades

NE Trades

SE Monsoon

Doldrums

Doldrums

Doldrums

SE Trades

SE Trades

SE Trades

Roaring Forties

Top: The major wind systems of the world which were used by the clippers to travel the world in the age of sail.

Above: A square-rigged barque.

Right: Sail adjustment of a square rigged boat to catch the wind.

wind

Fore-and-aft rig

Fore-and-aft rig existed in the middle-east long before it was used in the west. This vessel is an Arab dhow.

Fore-and-aft rig is so-called because the sails can be set not only at right-angles to the vessel's centre-line, as with square rig, but also almost in line with it, from *forward* to *aft*.

The sails of a vessel thus rigged can catch a wind not only coming from astern or from the side, but also one coming from diagonally ahead, and so can sail diagonally against the wind. This obviously increases a sailing vessel's range of direction enormously.

Fore-and-aft rigged vessels such as the dhows and feluccas of the eastern Mediterranean and Indian Ocean have been in existence for thousands of years. Why, then, in view of its obvious advantages, was this rig not adopted more rapidly and widely by the western world?

The answer is mainly to do with size. The eastern vessels remained comparatively small while those of the west became bigger and bigger, and fore-and-aft rig is a small-ship rig. Ships of the great age of sail in the western world, for example the ships of the Dutch East India Company, were huge, and even the ocean 'greyhounds', the clippers, which carried cargoes of tea and wool home to Europe and America from India and Australasia, were big. These vessels made the most of their enormous area of sail by using the wind-systems of

11

the world to reach their destinations instead of trying to sail there more directly.

The men who designed and sailed these ships were aware of the value of fore-and-aft rig, and made as much use of it as they could. Most big ships used to set fore-and-aft sails at their bow and stern, and sometimes midships as well.

Fore-and-aft rig is so much more efficient for smaller vessels that, after the big sailing ships had had their day, the western world accepted it completely. Today everything under sail, with the exception of a few training ships and the occasional yacht, is fore-and-aft rigged.

This beautiful four-master is almost entirely fore-and-aft rigged. She is the Chilean training ship Esmeralda.

Variations of fore-and-aft rig

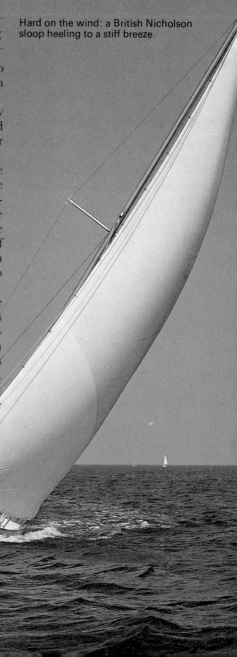

Hard on the wind: a British Nicholson sloop heeling to a stiff breeze.

Fore-and-aft rig can be divided into various categories, each with its own special name.

These categories depend basically on two things: the number and position of the vessel's masts, and her *working rig*.

A vessel's working sails are those she normally sets – in other words the sails which usually propel her, excluding any others hoisted to increase or maintain speed. Sometimes the normal sail area is reduced because of bad weather or for some other reason such as the ship edging her way into an anchorage.

The main reason for having more than one mast is to divide a vessel's total sail area into smaller and therefore more manageable units, which makes the work of handling the sails easier, especially in bad weather. Obviously this requirement does not apply to very small craft, so these rarely have more than one mast.

Una rig (lugsail rig)

The simplest possible rig for a sailing craft consists of one mast and one sail. This is called catboat rig in the United States, lugsail rig in Britain, and also, in the international world of sailing, Una rig, *una* derived from the Latin word meaning *one*. With Una rig, the mast has to be positioned well forward, almost up in the bows of the boat.

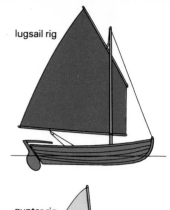

lugsail rig

Various types of fore-and-aft rig.

gunter rig

loose-footed gaff rig (Norfolk wherry)

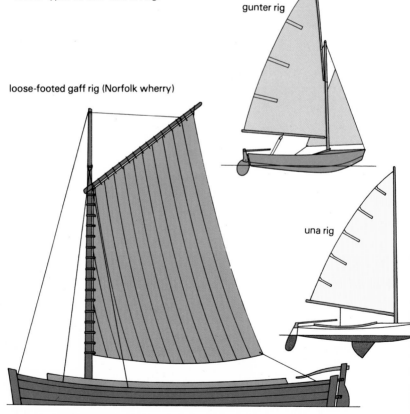

una rig

14

Boats with one mast and a single sail were once used widely for commercial purposes, for example for fishing off the east coast of America and for carrying timber, peat and other local produce on the inland waterways of eastern England. Nor is this rig by any means obsolete. Quite a number of modern dinghies, some of them highly efficient racing machines, are Una-rigged.

Sloop rig

The next-simplest rig comprises one mast and two sails. The mast is further back than in a Una-rigged boat, and will have one sail in front of it and one behind it. The sail behind the mast will be the larger, and is therefore called the *mainsail*. The sail in front of the mast is called the *jib*. A boat with this rig is said to be sloop-rigged, or a sloop.

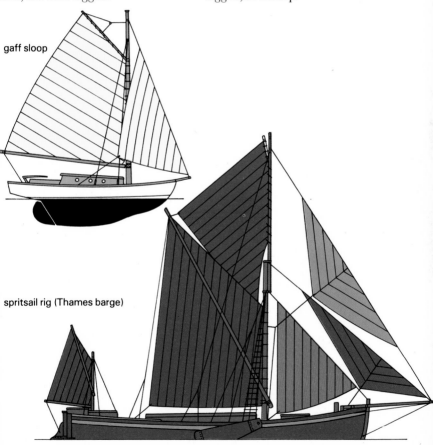

gaff sloop

spritsail rig (Thames barge)

Cutter rig

Some boats have a mainsail, like a sloop's, but have two sails in front of the mast instead of one. The mast may be positioned further back than in a sloop and the outer sail rigged to a spar extending from the bow – a *bowsprit*. Such a boat is said to be cutter-rigged, or a cutter.

Yawls, ketches and schooners

If a boat has two masts and three sails, definition is not quite so easy. It depends on the height and position of the rear mast. If this is very short and further back than the rear end of the boat's waterline (the level on the hull to which the water reaches), she is yawl-rigged, or a *yawl*. If this second mast is further forward than the rear end of the waterline and reasonably tall, though still shorter than the forward mast, the boat is ketch-rigged, or a *ketch*. If the rear mast is positioned further forward still and taller than the forward mast, the vessel is a *schooner*.

Yawls, ketches and schooners may carry the same headsails, that is, sails in front of the forward mast, as sloops and cutters. On yawls and ketches, the shorter, after mast is called the *mizzen mast*, and the sail hoisted on it, the *mizzen sail*. In schooners, the after mast, being the taller of the two, becomes the *mainmast*, and the sail hoisted on it the *mainsail*. The forward mast is known as the *foremast*, and the sail hoisted on its after side (the side towards the stern) is called the *foresail*.

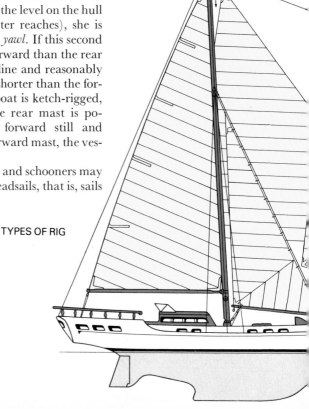

schooner

TYPES OF RIG

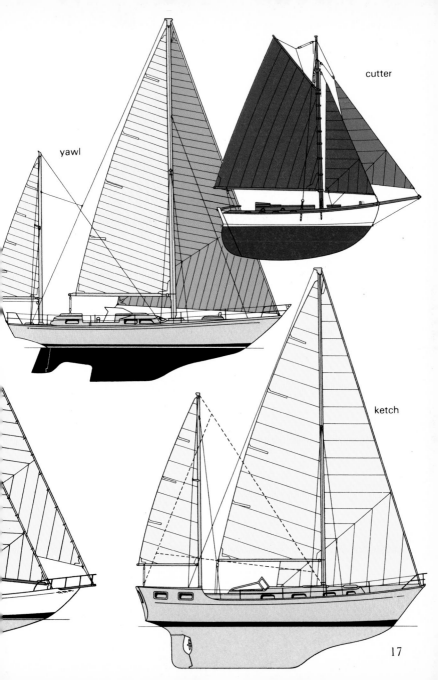

yawl

cutter

ketch

17

Sail shape

Just one more variation of rig should be noted, namely, the shape of the sails. All the sails hoisted in front of the vessel's mast or masts will be triangular. Those hoisted on the after side of a mast may be triangular or four-sided. If the sail is four-sided, it will need a pole (*spar*) across the top to extend it. When the pole is not attached to the mast at one end, but is suspended from the mast at some point along the spar, it is called *lug-sail* rig. If the forward end of the spar is attached to the mast (by a device permitting it to slide up and down), it will, when it is hoisted, either be very nearly perpendicular, like an extension of the mast itself, or slope up aft at a marked angle to the mast, the angle depending on the shape of the sail.

The very-nearly-perpendicular rig is called *gunter rig*, and a sloop with this kind of mainsail will be a gunter-rigged sloop. The pole-at-an-angle is called a *gaff*, so this is known as *gaff rig*. A cutter with this kind of mainsail is a gaff-rigged cutter.

There has been a marked tendency in recent times towards a simplification of sailing craft design and rig, and this has resulted in a triangular mainsail with no pole at the top at all. This rig, which the Americans call *Marconi* or *jib-headed*, and the British *Bermudan rig*, has almost completely replaced gaff and gunter rig. Gunter rig is now mostly confined to very small boats, one of its assets being that the mast and other poles can be short enough for easy transport, on the roof of a car, for instance, or in the bottom

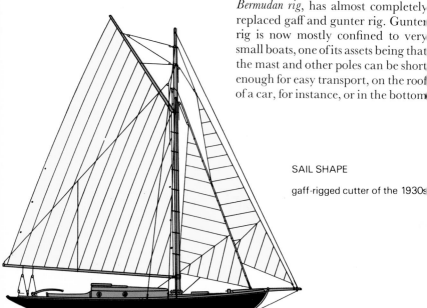

SAIL SHAPE

gaff-rigged cutter of the 1930s

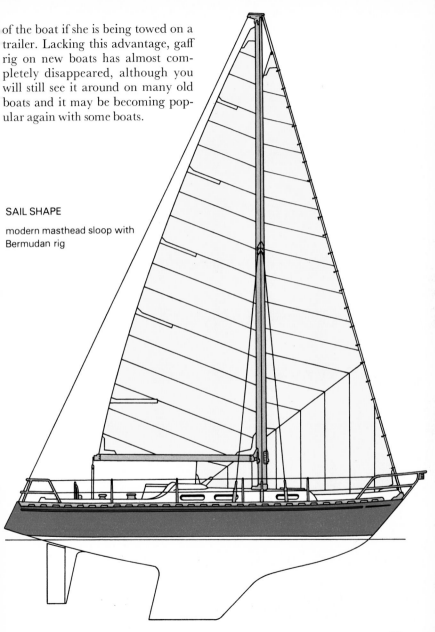

of the boat if she is being towed on a trailer. Lacking this advantage, gaff rig on new boats has almost completely disappeared, although you will still see it around on many old boats and it may be becoming popular again with some boats.

SAIL SHAPE

modern masthead sloop with Bermudan rig

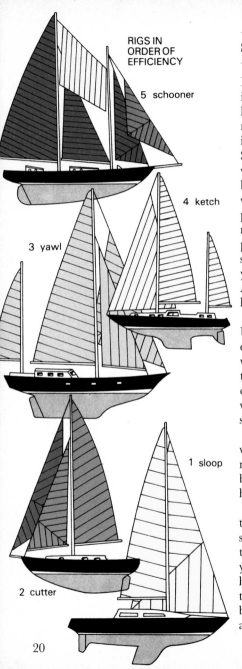

RIGS IN
ORDER OF
EFFICIENCY

5 schooner

4 ketch

3 yawl

1 sloop

2 cutter

Sailing performance

How efficient are the various categories of boat – sloops, cutters, yawls, ketches and schooners – as sailing machines? (They are described here in ascending order of performance.) Schooners are magnificent with the wind blowing from astern or the side, but not so good against it, which is what really counts in short-distance pleasure sailing. Whether you are racing or simply sailing, you can expect to be sailing against the wind some of the time, and that is when your true progress can be assessed. Also, schooner rig is only suitable for larger boats.

The eastern seaboard of the United States offers suitable coastal cruising conditions for schooners, which may quite frequently be seen there in all their glory. Around the coasts of Britain, where against-the-wind sailing is so common, the schooner is rare.

Next, the ketch. This is better to windward than the schooner, but not much. The ketch is a good cruising boat, her divided sail-plan making her easy to handle.

Then the yawl, which is better than the ketch against the wind. Like schooner-rig, yawl-rig is most suited to larger boats. There are some tiny yawls around with pocket-handkerchief mizzen sails whose contribution to the boat's progress must be more than offset by the wind resistance of the masts and rigging that are carrying them.

Next are the single-masted rigs, the cutter and the sloop. Cutters made a name for themselves as magnificent sea-boats – which is a sailor's way of saying they are very good at coping

Beating to windward. Sailing a high-performance dinghy can be exhilarating.

with rough weather. Cutters used to remain at sea for days under sail, alone in the stormy waters of the Bristol Channel, to put pilots aboard vessels inward-bound to the ports of South Wales and to take pilots off other outward-bound ships. Pilots steer ships into or out of harbours, or through difficult waters.

But for most of us, sailing is a much less rugged business than that. It is a leisure activity usually confined to sheltered or semi-sheltered waters. What we want is a boat which will take us round the buoys if we are racing, or perhaps up the coast and back for a day's sail or a cruise. This means we want a boat which will perform well on all points of sailing, and particularly against the wind.

Here the sloop has all the advantages. It is the most efficient of all the rigs against the wind, and there are only two sails to cope with. It is also the rig with the widest size range, being suitable for all grades of craft from tiny dinghies up to large ocean-going yachts.

The overwhelming majority of sailing craft afloat today are sloops, so this is the type which will be examined in more detail.

The Sailing Machine

This chapter describes the main parts of a sailing boat.

The hull

The body of the boat is called the hull. The hull accommodates those on board, and from the hull the boat's movement through the water is controlled.

The very first man-made hulls were hollowed-out tree trunks, but there has been considerable progress since then. Many small modern sailing cruisers have gas stoves, electric lights, flush toilets, and so on.

The trouble with hollowing out a

Left: One of the earliest boats — a dug-out canoe hollowed out of a tree trunk and roughly streamlined at each end.
Below: Another primitive craft — a coracle, made by covering a wooden framework with skins.
Opposite, top: An Eskimo kayak. The design is centuries old, but startlingly like modern canoes.
Opposite, centre: Primitive dug-out canoes were moved by using spear-shaped paddles.
Opposite bottom: The old Eskimo kayak was made of skins and wood. The modern version is GRP, with an outboard engine!

tree trunk is that it imposes a limitation on size. Your boat can only be as long and as wide and as deep as the longest and thickest tree trunk available.

This limitation was overcome when someone had the bright idea of constructing a skeleton boat and covering this with a 'skin' of some sort. This also made the boat much lighter, more buoyant and consequently easier to control. Some of the earliest boats of this type were literally skeletons constructed from animal bones and covered with animal skins. The Eskimos used to have kayaks of this kind, but they too have progressed. Nowadays they have glass-fibre vessels with outboard motors.

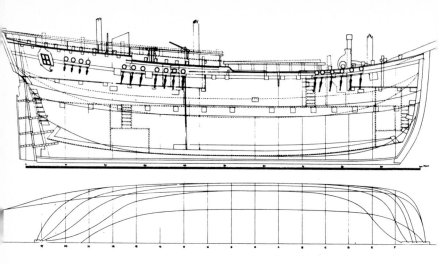

Wooden hulls

For centuries, all boats, and ships too, for that matter, were built of wood by fastening planking over a wooden framework. A large number of pleasure craft, from dinghies to some of the largest yachts afloat, are still constructed in this fashion.

The first stage in building a wooden ship or boat is to lay down the strong backbone called the *keel*. This is extended forwards and upwards by another strong timber called the *stem-post*, and aft by a similar one called the *stern-post*. To this assembly are attached, at right angles, the ribs which take the planking and the frames which strengthen the structure at certain points.

The wooden 'skin' may take one of several forms. If it consists of planks, these will run lengthwise, and if the planks are fastened on edge-to-edge, the vessel will be *carvel-built*. The

Plan of one of the most famous wooden ships of all time – Captain Cook's Endeavour, in which he sailed on his exploration of the world.

word 'carvel' comes from 'caravel', a small, fast European sailing ship of the 15th to 17th centuries which was planked in this fashion. Another method is to make each plank overlap the one below it, a form of construction sometimes used in building wooden houses. A boat planked this way is said to be *clinker-built*, or clench-built, because each plank clenches, or grips, the one below it.

Another way of laying on the 'skin' is to build it up from very thin sheets of wood glued one on top of the other, with the grain of each sheet running at an angle to that of the sheet below. This method is known as *moulded construction*. It gives a beautifully smooth and rounded result, but is suitable only for small boats.

Plywood This material (thin layers of wood glued together under pressure) is widely used in boat-building, not only for decks but for hulls as well. But it must be marine plywood. Marine plywood is produced specifically to withstand wet conditions and is therefore very suitable for the hulls of small boats, but it does have one big limitation, and that is that it will not bend in two planes at the same time, so it cannot be used for the traditionally rounded type of hull.

A basic plywood hull will have a flat side and a flat bottom, with a comparatively sharp angle where they meet. The joint thus formed is called a *chine*, a word meaning

DIFFERENT TYPES OF HULL CONSTRUCTION

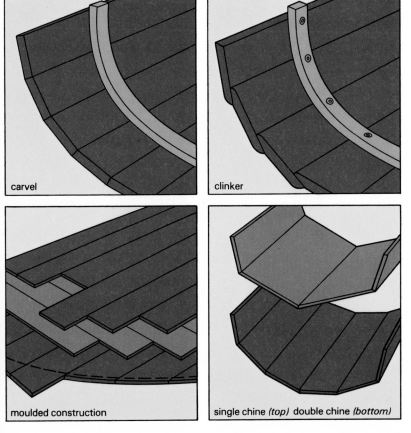

carvel

clinker

moulded construction

single chine *(top)* double chine *(bottom)*

a sharp ridge, and so a boat thus constructed is said to be hard-chined. In a very small boat there will probably be only one such joint on each side of the keel, and such a boat is said to be single-chined. In larger boats, the plywood skin may have several joints, with a chine between each pair of adjoining sheets. Such a hull will be defined as double-chined, treble-chined, or even multi-chined, as the case may be.

Plywood boats are not inferior boats. Their number includes many high-performance racing dinghies. Marine plywood is very strong for its weight, and it is by far the simplest form of 'planking' for the do-it-yourself boat builder. Proof of this is the almost bewildering number of designs for plywood boats which are available in kit form.

Metal hulls

You may occasionally see small sailing boats with metal hulls, though in number there are very few. A metal hull is constructed in much the same way as a wooden one, the skin in this case consisting of thin plates riveted, or, more often now, welded on to a metal frame. The metal used for the plates will be either steel or aluminium. Steel is really too heavy for anything smaller than a medium-sized yacht (more than 10 metres). Although one successful class of dinghy is planked, or rather plated, with aluminium, it is firstly too expensive, and secondly too much trouble to maintain, to be a sensible proposition

for the ordinary boat-owner to want to buy one.

Glass-fibre Reinforced Plastic (GRP) hulls

The biggest development in hull construction in recent years has been the introduction of GRP hulls. These are made in one piece by various moulding processes and are therefore very well suited to the mass-production methods which the present-day demand for small craft requires. GRP hulls are very strong, and there are no below-the-waterline seams to leak, as those of a wooden or metal boat may do. They also need less maintenance. In fact about the only thing that can be said against them is that GRP is not a particularly attractive material to live with. This may not matter in the case of a dinghy, which you are not aboard for very long, but it may at cruising boat level. GRP cruising hulls look bare inside and tend to feel cold and clammy, though this can easily be overcome by lining the boat or at least its accommodation area with something warmer such as canvas, hardboard, or wooden slats. If this is done, it is important to ensure adequate ventilation of the space behind the lining to avoid condensation being trapped.

Above, right: Boat-building has been transformed by the introduction of the GRP hull. Mould shown here.
Right: GRP yachts under construction at the Fairway Marine Company, England. GRP hulls are very strong, have no seams to leak, and also require little maintenance.

PARTS OF A DINGHY

1. mainsail
2. batten pocket
3. boom
4. clew outhaul
5. mainsheet jamming cleat
6. tiller extension
7. tiller
8. spinnaker sheet leads
9. rudder lift line
10. pintle and gudgeon assembly
11. rudder blade
12. toe straps
13. mainsheet traveller control line
14. mainsheet power block
15. mainsheet blocks
15a. mainsheet
16. mainsheet traveller
17. traveller track
18. centreboard case
19. centreboard
20. centreboard control line
21. kicking strap
22. mast step
23. mast
24. mainsail halyard
25. sliding gooseneck
26. luff groove
27. jib
28. forestay
29. bow fitting
30. jib sheets
31. shroud
32. shroud lanyard
33. shroud plate
34. built-in buoyancy

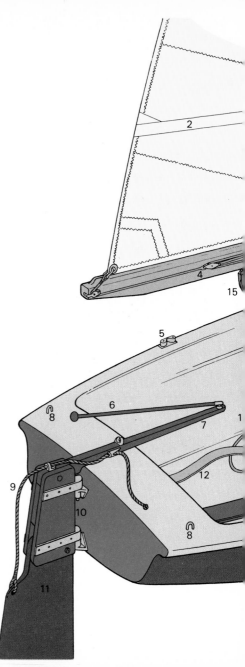

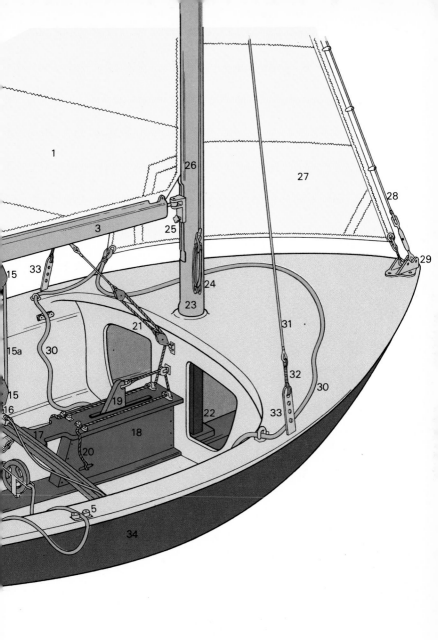

1

26

27

3

25

28

15   33

24

23

29

21

31

15a   30

32

19

30

15

22

33

16

17

18

20

5

34

Hull shape

Hulls vary considerably in shape, especially at the ends, and particularly at the stern. The bow, seen from the side, may be curved or straight. Seen from the front, it may come to a point, or its upper part may be blanked off with a flat board. This makes it look as though the actual point of the bow has been cut off, and is in fact called a 'sawn-off' bow. This type of bow is a dinghy characteristic and is done to facilitate construction and also to make the boat more compact.

As far as the stern is concerned, this may be blanked off in much the same way as a sawn-off bow. A flat, vertical or almost vertical stern like this is called a *transom stern*, and is the one

most commonly found in small craft. Some sterns taper up at a shallow angle from the waterline almost to a sharp edge. This is called a *counter*, and is a feature of older boats. A modification of this is to blank off the taper at some stage, producing a sawn-off counter. Some boats have a stern sloping forward instead of aft. This is a *reverse counter* and is a common feature of modern racing yachts.

Left: Conventional pointed bow, sloping up with a very slight curve.
Above: A long, overhanging stern is a characteristic of older boats.
Above, right: A modern design with a sawn-off counter. This increases space aft, an advantage in a cruising boat.
Right: The shape of this stern is called a reverse counter, and is essentially a racing feature.

Dimensions The characteristics of a boat's hull are summarised by four measurements. These are: her maximum length at deck level, which is called her Length Over All (abbreviated to LOA); her normal length on the waterline, which is called her Load Waterline Length (abbreviated to LWL); her width at her widest part, which is called her beam; and her depth in the water, which is called her draught. Two figures may be given for the draught and these will be explained later.

These dimensions can tell us a lot about a larger boat without it being seen. The difference between her LOA and her LWL represents her *overhangs*, the amount by which her bow and stern together overhang the water. If this difference is considerable, and in addition her beam is less than a third of her LWL, she will almost certainly be an old boat with poor accommodation for her size, and a wet one to sail because she will tend to cut through the water rather than ride over it. If she has virtually no overhangs, she is again likely to be an old boat, perhaps with plenty of room inside her, but slow and heavy to handle. Modern boats have moderate overhangs and are very broad in the beam compared with the old-timers, which gives modern boats good accommodation and the buoyancy to ride the waves instead of ploughing through them.

Where dinghies are concerned, there may be very little difference between the LOA and the LWL. The most significant dimension in the case of these little boats is the beam. Generally speaking, the 'beamier' (wider) the boat, the more advanced the design will be.

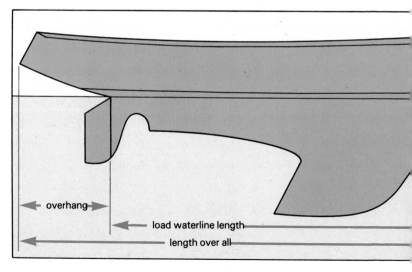

overhang

load waterline length

length over all

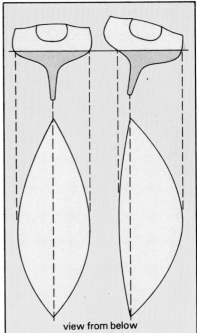

Above: This heeling boat shows how the Load Waterline Length increases in such a position. As the hull tilts, the waterline moves to a higher point on its side.

Right: LWL increases when the boat is heeled because more of the overhangs are submerged.

Below: The principal dimensions of a boat.

view from below

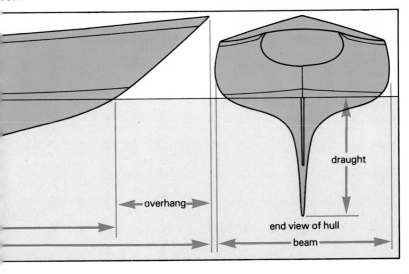
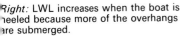

overhang

draught

end view of hull

beam

Multi-hulls

Multi-hulls are, as the term indicates, boats with more than one hull. Although of ancient origin, this design has only recently been used for yachts.

There are two main types: the catamaran and the trimaran. The catamaran, or 'cat' as it is usually called, is the more common of the two designs.

Catamarans These have two identical hulls connected by strong cross members. They range from dinghy length to ocean-going craft of considerable size, some of the bigger ones having very roomy, comfortable accommodation built over the deck beams on a connecting platform. They can be rigged in various ways, but as with the more conventional mono-hull craft, the majority are sloops. The hulls are usually constructed of plywood or GRP. They are very shallow-draught craft, which makes them particularly suitable for shoal (shallow) waters.

Because of the great beam provided by their two, spaced hulls, catamarans are more stable than single-hulled boats. They heel over less and they set up less water-resistance, so they are among the fastest sailing craft afloat today. Smallish 'cats', a stage or two up from dinghy-size, have been timed as doing upwards of 30 kilometres per hour.

Sailing a catamaran in a fresh breeze is truly exhilarating. The acceleration in particular is so terrific that you may feel you are taking off!

Catamarans have twin hulls and usually the same rig as dinghies. They are fast and exciting boats to sail.

Catamarans do have one serious disadvantage. It is a double disadvantage in that they *can* capsize, and they are not self-righting. Except in the most extreme conditions a single-hulled cabin boat with a conventional ballast keel will not capsize, and if she *should* suffer a knockdown (be knocked flat on the water by a sudden violent gust of wind), she will, unless she is almost instantly swamped, right herself. Dinghies can also usually be righted by their crews after a capsize. A catamaran, if she goes over, will stay there. If she is dinghy-size, her crew may just be able to right her, but if she is any larger than that, help will almost certainly be necessary.

A catamaran may not just be knocked flat either. She may turn completely upside-down. To prevent his happening, some catamarans carry on top of the mast what looks like a small flying saucer, but which is in fact a buoyancy chamber. Another safeguard is to reduce the sail area early when sailing in a strong wind.

Trimarans As the name indicates, trimarans have three hulls, a main one in the centre, flanked by two smaller ones. Materials and methods of construction are much the same as for catamarans, and they have the same advantages of stability and speed – the same disadvantages, too, in the event of a capsize. In size they range from dinghy-style 'babies' to large ocean-going yachts. A number of trimarans have made a name for themselves in deep-sea cruising and racing.

Below: Trimarans range from dinghy-size to large yachts.
Inset: A buoyancy chamber at the top of a catamaran's mast prevents a total capsize.

Keels

The word 'keel' is used in two senses where boats are concerned. Firstly it is the backbone of a boat built in the conventional fashion, and secondly – and this is most people's idea of a keel – it is a downward-projection from the underside of the boat. The second type could be termed a 'sailing keel'.

What is the purpose of this kind of keel? Power boats do not have them – only sailing boats. Why?

The answer is simple. It is to prevent the boat being pushed sideways by the wind.

You can do a simple experiment using a bowl of water to see how the keel works. Cup your hand upwards and let it lie on the surface of the water like a boat's hull. Move it sideways, and you will find the water offers very little resistance.

Now flatten your hand. Immerse it in the water vertically, and again move it sideways. You will find the resistance of the water greatly increased.

This is exactly how a boat's keel works – by building up water-resistance to the sideways thrust of the wind.

Ballast keels

There are various kinds of sailing keel. Many larger boats have their sailing keel built as a part of the underwater profile of the hull. Such keels will usually be partly or wholly made of some very heavy material such as lead (extremely expensive nowadays), or iron, or even concrete. This enables them to perform a double function: to withstand the sideways thrust of the wind as described earlier; and to provide a heavy weight low down which, as the boat heels over, will exert a force to right her again. The further she heels over, the greater this leverage will be. This is the safety factor which enables a boat to recover from a knock-down.

Keels of this kind are called ballast keels because they perform the same function as ballast in a ship, which provides a weight low down to keep the vessel upright.

Fin keels

These keels look rather like a fish's fin, and are attached to, but not built

A traditional yacht with the ballast keel a part of the hull and the rudder mounted on the transom stern.

into, the hull of the boat. Their function is to withstand the sideways thrust of the wind rather than to exert a righting effect, which is achieved in other ways. Because they are much shorter than built-in keels and therefore offer less resistance to the water, fin keels tend to be a feature of racing or high-performance craft. They are also mainly a characteristic of larger boats, though one or two smaller designs do have them.

Bilge keels

Some boats have twin keels fitted on either side of the centre-line of the hull. These are called bilge keels. The bilge of a boat is, generally speaking, that part of her hull which is below the waterline, and bilge keels are fitted just below the point at which

Right: A modern boat with a fin keel and a skeg rudder. Although good for performance, both are easily damaged.

KEEL SHAPES

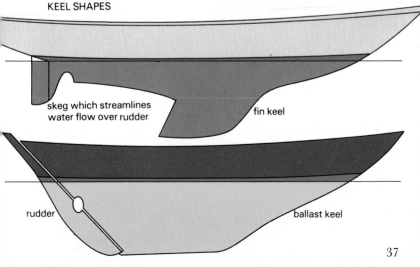

skeg which streamlines
water flow over rudder

fin keel

rudder

ballast keel

the side of the boat turns a corner (either smoothly in the case of a round-section hull, or sharply in the case of a hard-chine hull) and becomes the bottom.

Bilge keels have certain advantages. They reduce a vessel's draught because they are shorter than fin keels, and allow her to sit upright when out of the water, whether unintentionally when she goes aground on a sandbank or mudflat on a falling tide, or intentionally in some quiet spot for the night, or when she is laid up for the winter. A boat with a single, central keel would, unless supported, lie over to one side or the other. (Catamarans and trimarans will also sit up straight when out of the water, because of their double or triple hulls.)

A boat with bilge keels may also be steadier than a single-keeled boat, especially in rough weather, when her keels will have a similar effect to a ship's stabilizing fins. The objection to them is that they detract considerably from a boat's performance. Bilge keels are fine for cruising, but you will not find many bilge-keeled racing craft around.

Retractable keels

So far only fixed keels have been mentioned. Many boats, most of them at or near the bottom of the sailing boat size range, have retractable keels. In fact, since almost all dinghies have keels of this kind, there must be more boats afloat with retractable keels than any others.

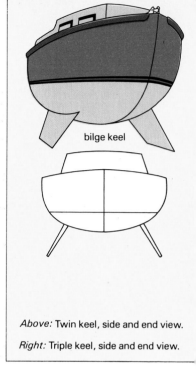

Above: Twin keel, side and end view.

Right: Triple keel, side and end view.

A retractable keel works through a slot on the centreline of the boat's hull. Around the slot is built a narrow casing to prevent the boat being flooded through it.

This is why some boats have two figures for their draught. They are boats with retractable keels. One figure is for their draught with the centreboard or dagger board (keel) lowered, and the other for when it is fully raised.

But – why have a retractable keel at all? There are a number of reasons. An incidental one is that if you sail in

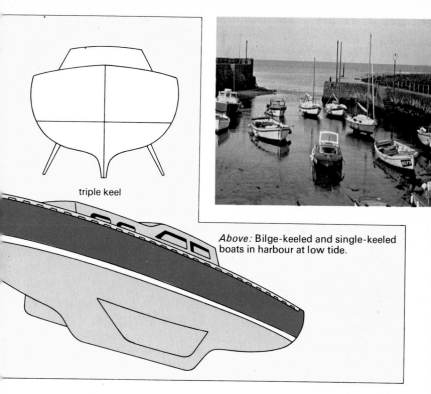

triple keel

Above: Bilge-keeled and single-keeled boats in harbour at low tide.

shoal waters with the keel down, its scraping the bottom will be a useful warning of when you are in danger of going aground. The main reasons are that retractable keels make transport and handling of the boat easier, and can improve sailing performance. Most boats with retractable keels are very small, the great majority of them dinghies, and such boats are not normally left afloat when not in use. This means they have frequently to be manhandled in or out of the sea, river, lake, gravel pit, or whatever the sailing area may be, and this is

obviously much easier to do if the keel can be retracted. Similarly, the boat can be parked or trailed more easily if there is no keel sticking out of the bottom.

The value of a retractable keel from the sailing point of view is that under certain circumstances it can be raised, either partially or completely, which will reduce the 'drag' of the boat through the water, and so increase her speed.

The keel can be adjusted to any position, from fully retracted to fully extended, and the ability to judge just how much keel to use under the conditions prevailing at the time is one of the marks of a good helmsman.

Centreboards If the keel is housed in a casing when retracted, it is called a centreboard. A centreboard has a pivot at its lower, forward corner and is raised or lowered by a tackle attached to the opposite corner.

Centreboards were once a common feature of boats of all sizes, but are rarely found now in anything much bigger than dinghies. This is because modern trends in sailing craft design have been towards greater simplicity and the removal of as many joints and moving parts as possible. Centreboard housings can leak and the boards themselves jam in them, especially if the boards have become bent or warped. Also, housings can take up valuable cabin space.

Dagger boards Some very small boats have what are known as dagger boards. These perform the same function as centreboards, but are much

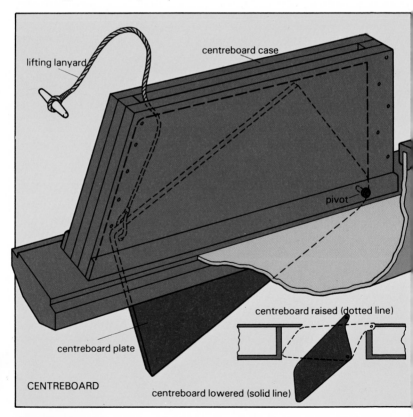

lifting lanyard

centreboard case

pivot

centreboard plate

centreboard raised (dotted line)

CENTREBOARD

centreboard lowered (solid line)

simpler, being basically flat plates or boards which are pushed straight down into an open-topped housing, built up above the waterline to prevent water entering the boat, and pulled straight up again, by hand. There is no pivotal arrangement. They are called dagger boards because pushing them down and pulling them out again is rather like sheathing and unsheathing a dagger. When they are not required dagger boards can be removed completely.

Removable keels should always be raised before the boat runs on to the beach. They should also be checked regularly for leaks in the casing and any damage. It is important that the keel is sound so that it can be used as a lever to right the boat if it capsizes.

Below, left: Centreboard mechanism.

Below, centre: Dagger board mechanism.

Below: Lowering a centreboard.

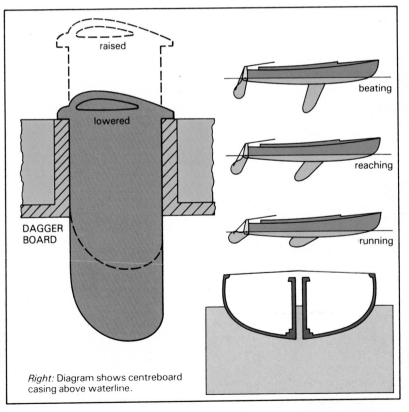

raised

lowered

DAGGER BOARD

beating

reaching

running

Right: Diagram shows centreboard casing above waterline.

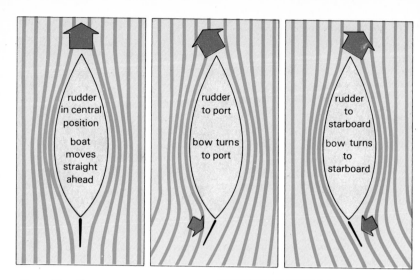

Above: The effect of the rudder on the water flow around the hull.

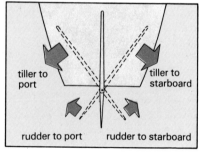

Right: The movement of the tiller affecting the rudder and altering the boat's direction.

Controlling the direction of the vessel

A rudder is another flat, vertical board or plate, like the sailing keel, and, like the keel, works by setting up resistance to the water the boat is sailing through. It is attached to the after end of the boat, pivoting at its forward edge so that it can be angled to the right or left (to starboard or

port), whichever is required.

If the rudder is in the central position, in line with the keel, the water just flows past it, and the boat moves straight ahead. If the rudder is angled to the right (starboard), the water builds up against it on the right, acting as a brake on that side of the boat so that it turns to the right. If it is angled to the left, the water builds up against it on the left-hand side of the boat, which will turn to the left.

In most small boats, the rudder will be operated by a tiller, which is simply a lever attached to the top of the rudder and usually made of wood. The principle of the lever is that its ends move in opposite directions, so if you move the tiller to the right, the rudder will be angled to the left, and the boat will turn left. Similarly, if you push the tiller over to the left, the rudder will be angled to the right, and the boat will turn to the right.

In larger boats, the rudder may be operated by a wheel. If this is the case, the wheel will be linked to the rudder in such a way that it acts like the steering wheel of a car. If you turn the wheel to the right, the boat will turn to the right. If you turn it to the left, the boat will turn to the left. In other words, whichever way you turn the wheel, the boat will turn in the same direction.

One big difference between steering a car and a boat is that, whereas any movement of the steering wheel of a car will result in an instant change of direction, a boat may take anything from a moment to several seconds to answer her helm – in other words, for the effect of the rudder to make itself felt. This time-lapse may be negligible in the case of a nippy little dinghy, but with a big boat it will be an important element in handling her safely, especially if there is not much room to manoeuvre.

This is a good point to repeat that in sailing language the right-hand side is starboard and the left-hand side port.

So far only the body of a boat and the attachments which permit it to maintain and change direction have been mentioned. Now let us go on to what actually makes a sailing boat go – the sails, together with all their attachments.

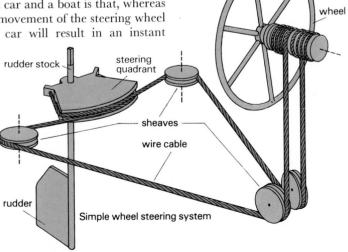

wheel

rudder stock

steering quadrant

sheaves

wire cable

rudder

Simple wheel steering system

Spars and standing rigging

As already described a sailing boat is propelled by the force of the wind on her sails. These are supported and in certain cases extended by spars – some have already been referred to, most un-nautically, as 'poles'.

Modern sailing craft may have one or more of three kinds of spar. The main spar or spars will be the mast or masts, which support the sails. Most will also have horizontal spars stretching out the foot of the sails hoisted on the after side of their masts. These spars are called *booms*, the one on the mainmast being the main boom and the one on the mizzen mast, if the craft is a yawl or a ketch, the mizzen boom, and so on. When the light-weather sail known as a spinnaker is in use, this will be extended by a spinnaker boom.

Some boats will also have the tops of the sails aft of the mast extended by a spar, as in the case of gaff and gunter rig.

All spars were once made of wood. Nowadays they may be wood, or metal (light alloy), or glass-fibre.

Stays

Where masts are concerned, most of these will be supported by wire stays which are rigged once the mast has been *stepped* (put up). A few small boats have unstayed masts which may be flexible. In sensitive and capable hands a flexible, or *bendy*, mast is considered to improve a boat.

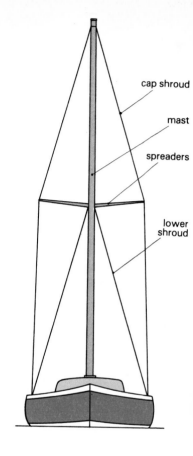

cap shroud

mast

spreaders

lower shroud

The great majority of boats will have a single mast stayed in the following manner.

There will be one stay running from the bow of the boat to the top of the mast, or a point near it. Because this stay is in front of, or before, the mast, it is called the *forestay*.

The mast will also be supported from the side by twin stays or sets of stays running from a point or points

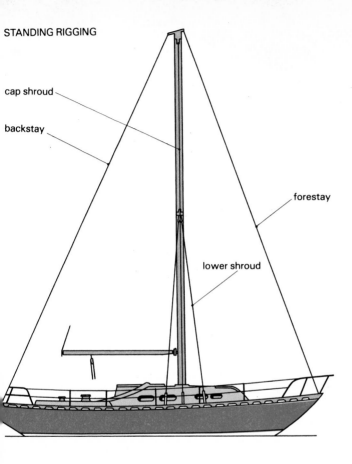

cap shroud

backstay

forestay

lower shroud

abreast of the mast up to, or near, its top. These sideways stays are called *shrouds*.

In some boats the mast may also be supported from aft, either by a centre stay or by twin stays running back to either side of the stern. These are *backstays*. This support from aft is not often found in very small boats because it is not necessary, and backstays might foul the main sail.

The stays described here constitute the boat's standing rigging (there may of course be others on a big boat, especially if she has more than one mast). They are called 'standing' rigging because, once they have been set up for the season's sailing, they are usually left like that, apart from necessary replacements or adjustments, until the boat is dismantled again.

Sails and running rigging

The boat which we are using as an example is, of course, a sloop, which means she has a working rig of two sails, the mainsail and the jib.

Taken together, the mainsail and jib form the boat's sail-plan, and their relative sizes must be carefully calculated, in connection with other factors such as hull shape and mast position, so that they balance each other. If the jib is too large, the bow can easily be blown round away from the wind (lee helm) and the helmsman will have to fight this. Ideally the sail balance should be such that the boat has a slight tendency to turn towards the wind (weather helm – see page 66) and this can be a safety factor.

Most sloops are Bermudan-rigged, which means that both their sails are triangular. This is the simplest of the two-sail rigs, and the one described.

The sides and corners of the two sails have names, the same in both cases. The top corner of the jib and the mainsail is the *head*, the bottom forward corner the *tack*, and the bottom after corner the *clew*. The forward edge of the sail is the *luff*, the after edge the *leech*, and the bottom edge the *foot*.

The leech of a conventional Bermudan mainsail has a number of narrow pockets sewn in at right-angles to

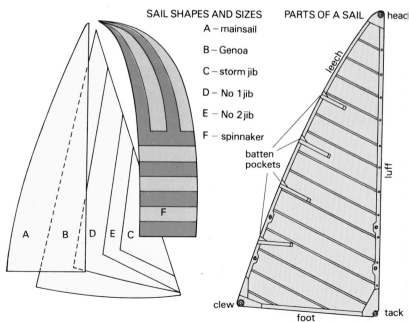

SAIL SHAPES AND SIZES

A – mainsail

B – Genoa

C – storm jib

D – No 1 jib

E – No 2 jib

F – spinnaker

batten pockets

PARTS OF A SAIL

head

leech

luff

clew

foot

tack

t, into which are slipped lath-like trips of wood or plastic. These are he sail *battens*, and their job is to extend or stiffen the leech so that the sail will set properly. The leech is slightly curved, and without battens he sail would tend to fold over along a direct line from head to clew.

Some sails have battens running heir entire width, and are therefore aid to be fully-battened. These full-length battens are thought to give the sail a curve which makes it more effective, especially in light winds. Fully-battened sails are most commonly found on multi-hulls (catamarans and trimarans), and very small racing craft, especially a number of Una-rig designs. They are also a feature of Australian boats.

When a sloop's sails are hoisted, he luff of the jib usually runs up the forestay, to which it is attached at ntervals by clips, rather like a curtain sliding along a wire. The luff of he mainsail is also attached to the mast by a sliding system which varies according to the size of the craft. One of the most common methods, at least for larger craft, is for the luff to have slides attached to it at intervals and hese run up and down a track on the mast.

The foot of the mainsail will normally be extended by a boom, to which it may be attached, perhaps by slides in the same way that the luff is attached to the mast. If the foot of the sail is not attached to the boom along ts length, but only held at the clew, he sail is said to be *loose-footed*.

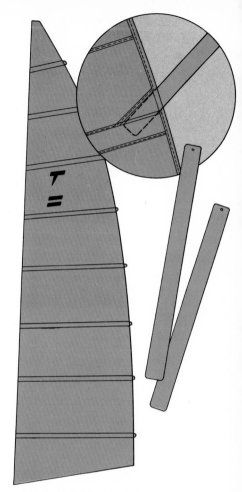

FULLY BATTENED MAINSAIL
(as used on Tornado catamaran)

Inset: Batten is inserted into leech of mainsail through an angled sleeve leading to the batten pocket itself

47

Running rigging

A boat's running rigging comprises the wires and ropes by which the sails are hoisted and controlled. It is called running rigging because it runs through *blocks* (pulleys) and other devices such as fairleads (eyes), which alter the direction of 'pull' of a rope.

The sails are hoisted by *halyards* (haul-yards), and the ropes that control the sail are called sheets. The jib has two sheets to enable it to be set on either side of the mast. Hauling on either will pull the jib over to that side of the boat. The mainsail has only one sheet, usually attached to the after end of the boom.

The halyards for both the mainsail

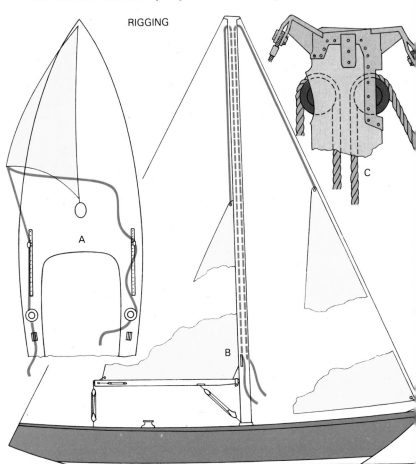

RIGGING

48

and the jib start at the foot of the mast, run up to a sheave (built into the mast head) or a block (attached to the mast) which they pass through and then fall back down and are attached to the head of the sail.

In each corner of the sail, at the main attachment points, are small circular holes usually metal-rimmed to prevent chafe on the sail fabric. These are called *cringles*. The usual method of attachment is by using a *shackle*. This is a U-shaped metal fitment with a removable pin across its open end. The attachment is made by removing the pin, slipping the open shackle through the cringle and the eye of the halyard, and replacing the

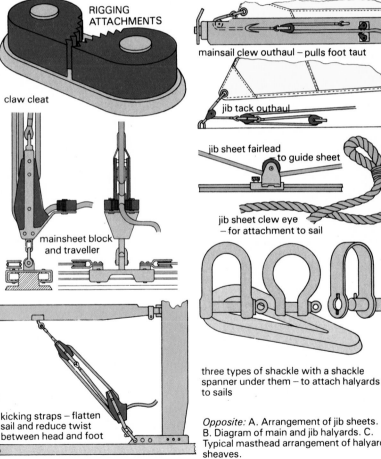

RIGGING ATTACHMENTS

claw cleat

mainsheet block and traveller

kicking straps – flatten sail and reduce twist between head and foot

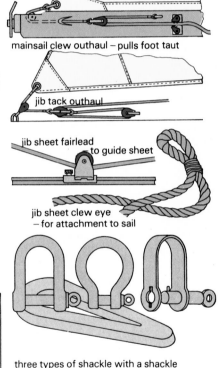

mainsail clew outhaul – pulls foot taut

jib tack outhaul

jib sheet fairlead – to guide sheet

jib sheet clew eye – for attachment to sail

three types of shackle with a shackle spanner under them – to attach halyards to sails

Opposite: A. Arrangement of jib sheets. B. Diagram of main and jib halyards. C. Typical masthead arrangement of halyard sheaves.

49

pin through the shackle. Once the sails are attached to their halyards, they can be hoisted.

Bending on the sails

When bending on (attaching) the sails, deal with the mainsail first. On a boat where the luff and foot of the mainsail have slides working along tracks on the mast and boom respectively, slip the slides on the foot of the sail into the track on the boom, starting from the forward end, and secure the tack of the sail to the forward end by means of a shackle passing through the tack cringle. Then pull the foot of the sail taut by means of the *outhaul* (a line), which should already be attached to the clew cringle, and make this fast round the cleat on the after end of the boom.

Now proceed similarly with the luff, inserting the slides, starting at the top of the sail, into the bottom of the mast track. There will usually be a device called a gate to prevent these slipping out again.

The sail is then attached to the halyard as already described. The mainsheet should already be attached to the boom.

Bending on the jib is simpler. Attach the tack of the sail to the bow fitting of the boat. A snap shackle may be used for this purpose, or the kind previously described. The jib halyard is attached to the head of the sail in a similar manner. Finally, attach the jib sheets, usually a continuous length of rope with an eye splice at the mid-point where the attach-

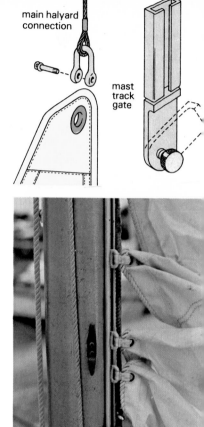

Above: Mainsail slides in mast track.

ment is made to the clew of the sail. The jib sheets are led down the port and starboard sides of the boat respectively to points convenient for their handling by the crew.

When the sails are hoisted, it is most important, if the mainsail is to set properly, that the foot is stretched

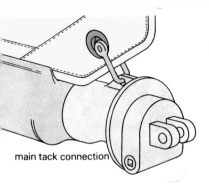

main tack connection

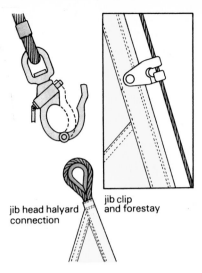

jib head halyard connection

jib clip and forestay

Above: Using halyard winch to tension halyard.

out tightly, and equally that the luffs of both the jib and the mainsail are as taut as possible. Any slack on either will seriously affect the boat's performance.

The next step is to go for a short trip, but to do that, something must be known of the principles of sailing.

Below: Putting jib luff clips on to forestay.

Below: Kicking strap which holds boom down.

Principles of Sailing

Provided weather conditions are reasonable, and there are no navigational hazards in her way, a fore-and-aft-rigged sailing vessel should be able to go anywhere she wishes. If the wind is 'free' in the nautical sense, that is, in her favour, she can sail directly to her destination. And even if she wants to go right up to windward, in other words just where the wind is blowing from, she should be able to get there, though she will have to do so indirectly and it will take a lot longer than it would have done if the wind was behind her or on the beam (coming from the side).

Points of sailing

The direction in which a sailing boat is moving relative to the wind is called her point of sailing, and there are, broadly speaking, three of these. When she is sailing with the wind behind her, she is said to be *running*. When she is sailing with the wind coming from the side, she is *reaching*. And when she is sailing with the wind coming from ahead, she is *beating*.

These three points of sailing merge into each other. It is impossible to say precisely when one ends and the other begins. For example if the wind is coming almost at right-angles to the boat's course but just slightly behind, a boat may be said to be on a broad reach, because the angle between her course and the direction of the wind is more than a right-angle. With the wind coming from a few degrees further behind, she will be running, while with it coming from a few degrees ahead of the beam, she will be on a close reach, because the angle between her course and the wind will be less than a right-angle. If the wind draws more directly ahead, the close reach will become a beat.

This is really only terminology. What matters is to know how to trim the sails to get the best out of them, wherever the wind is coming from. There are, however, basic requirements for each point of sailing.

Running

To repeat, a boat is running when the wind is coming from behind. This was the wind that suited those early sailing vessels which could only set their sails more or less squarely across their fore-and-aft line, so, when running, the mainsheet is slackened off until the mainsail is roughly at right-angles to the fore-and-aft line of the boat. The pressure of the wind on the sails will be transmitted as a force at right-angles to the sails (straight ahead), thus pushing the boat forwards.

Set like this, the mainsail will 'blanket' the jib, preventing the wind from filling it. The jib will either hang limp or flap about. There is no reason against sailing like this because you will be making headway, but if you want to move faster without putting up another sail, you can try 'goose-winging'. This means setting the jib on the other side of the boat from the mainsail. To do this for any length of time, you will probably need to hold out the foot of the jib using a spar, with the spar's outboard end attached to the clew of the sail, and its inner end secured to the mast. A spar used for this purpose is sometimes called a *whisker pole*.

If you are racing, you should hoist a spinnaker, if you have one. And if the boat has a retractable keel, you may raise this either wholly or partially, since it will not be required to counter any sideways thrust by the wind. There is, however, something else you may have to take into consideration in this respect, especially if you are sailing on the sea. A wind blowing from the side will tend to steady the boat, but a wind blowing from astern does not have this effect. As a result, steering is more difficult when running than on either of the other points of sailing. The boat will tend to yaw – her bows will try to swing from side to side. To counter this, you may find it advisable to keep the keel wholly or partially lowered, to give the hull a better grip in the water.

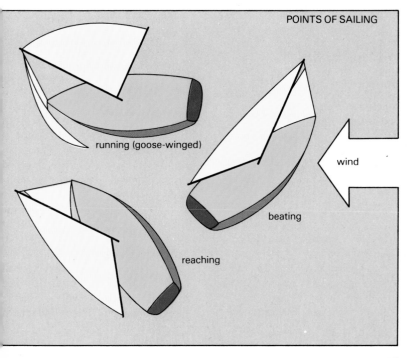

POINTS OF SAILING

running (goose-winged)

wind

beating

reaching

Helmsmanship Running is the most difficult point of sailing from the helmsman's point of view, so this is a suitable point at which to say a little more about helmsmanship in general.

The helmsman's most important job is to ensure that the boat is at all times moving through the water. This is called *steerage-way*. The rudder acts by creating water-resistance on one side of the boat or the other, but if the boat is not moving through the water, there will be no such resistance. The rudder will have no effect, and the boat will not be under control.

The helmsman should make major alterations of course with firmness and decision. Otherwise, since the action of the rudder exerts a braking effect and therefore slows the boat

Running before the wind with the mainsail boom almost at right-angles to the boat, and the jib goosewinged.

down, he or she should use it as little as possible.

Boats vary a great deal as regards how easy or difficult they are to steer especially the larger ones. Some require only a light hand on the helm while steering others can be really hard work. Some will keep a straight course almost of their own accord. Some will always try to turn towards the wind – which can be an advantage if the tiller is left unattended (see page 66) – and some away from it.

Gybing Running before the wind can be a very tricky business, with one possibility that must always be borne in mind, especially if the wind is strong. This is that the boat may 'gybe'. This happens when the boat is yawing, or the helmsman is not paying sufficient attention to the course, so that as the boat turns slightly the wind moves round to the side and thus to the forward or 'wrong' side of the mainsail and slams it and the boom right across the boat. All sorts of things can happen then. The boat may be dismasted, or capsize. The helmsman or someone else on board could be knocked overboard as the boom swings across.

So far we have been talking about an unintentional gybe. An intentional gybe is, however, a perfectly acceptable manoeuvre. Gybing is a common tactic when racing, and a necessity when picking up someone who has fallen overboard, because it is the quickest way of turning round and heading back the way you have come.

If the wind is not too strong, a boat may be allowed to gybe naturally. If it *is* strong, a controlled gybe is the answer. To do this, you haul in the mainsail and turn the boat to head towards the wind until, when the wind gets round on the wrong side of the sail, the boom will only have a short distance to travel. The sail can then be let out on the other side of the boat.

The way to avoid an unintentional gybe is to make sure the wind never gets round on to the wrong side of the mainsail, and the way to do that is to make sure the wind is always blowing at least a little from the side of the boat *opposite* that on which the sail is set. Sailing with the wind on the same side as that on which the sail is set is called 'sailing by the lee', and it can be very, very dangerous.

SAILING BY THE LEE

Wind is on same side of boat as sail is set.

GYBING

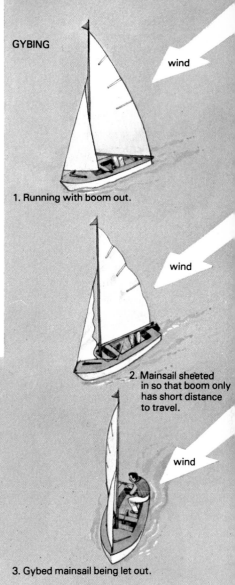

1. Running with boom out.

2. Mainsail sheeted in so that boom only has short distance to travel.

3. Gybed mainsail being let out.

Reaching

A sailing boat is reaching when the wind is coming sideways-on to her. On this point of sailing it will be necessary to haul the sails in closer than they are when running, but only to the degree where the wind will fill them. Since the pressure of the wind on a boat's sails results in a force transmitted at approximately 90° to the position of the sails, the less closely they are sheeted in, the more thrust there will be in an 'ahead' direction.

As a rough guide, if the wind is coming directly from either beam, at right-angles to the boat's course, the line of the sails will have to be angled at about 45° to her fore-and-aft line. If the wind is coming from further ahead than the beam, the sails will have to be sheeted in closer, and if it is coming from further astern, they can be let out more. If the sails are not sheeted in as closely as they should be, the wind will not fill them, or at least not properly, and either the boat will

not sail or she will sail more slowly than she could. If they are sheeted in too closely, the thrust of the wind will be transmitted in more of a sideways direction and again the boat will not make her best speed.

This is best illustrated by a simple manoeuvre. Suppose you are sailing with the wind behind you, which means you will have the sails out at right-angles to the boat. Now turn towards the wind until you have it on the beam, at right-angles to you. If you have not touched the sheets, the sails will be in line with the wind and will simply flutter without providing any propulsion at all. The boat will slow down, and, if you don't do anything about it, stop. If you sheet in the sails until they catch the wind, the boat will start moving again, until, when you have sheeted in the sails by just the right amount, she will be moving at her best speed in the prevailing conditions. But if you sheet in the sails too close, she will heel over

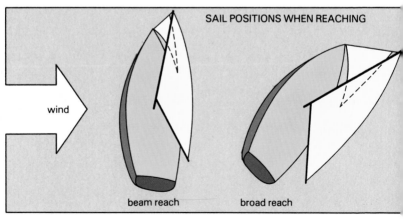

SAIL POSITIONS WHEN REACHING

wind

beam reach   broad reach

more and slow down, because too much of the thrust of the wind will be in a sideways direction. If you now let out the sheets, just enough, she will suddenly start to move again.

On a reach, the pressure of the wind on the sails, working as a lever against the resistance of the hull and keel in the water, will always tend to make a boat heel over. This can look very exciting, and sometimes it is. But a boat will sail fastest when she is upright, and this is why, when reaching, the crews of racing dinghies sit up on the *windward* side (the side the wind is coming from), or even sit out over the side on planks or trapezes, to do as much as they can to counteract the heel. This is not necessary with larger boats, most of which have heavy keels to exert a righting effect.

Above, right: Sailing on a fairly close reach. A little more into the wind, the reach would become a beat.
Below, right: Using trapezes to counteract the heel of the boat.

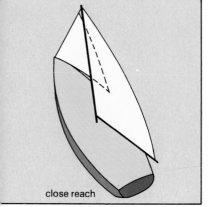

close reach

The balloon sail called a spinnaker may be used on a reach, on dinghies as well as larger boats. The latter may also put up another large sail when there is not too much wind. This is a sort of outsize jib known as a *Genoa*, or 'jenny'. Some Genoas are very large, larger even than the mainsail, which they will overlap. This sail is not as useful as a spinnaker on a run or a broad reach, but it has the advantage that it can still draw effectively when the boat is sailing quite close to the wind.

Reaching is the fastest and safest point of sailing. It is safest because it

Flying along, with both Genoa and spinnaker, on a reach.

gives you more scope for manoeuvring than the other points. You can turn towards the wind or away from it without anything drastic happening, unless you turn away so far that you get on to a run and then into a gybe, which should be easy enough to avoid.

As for its being the fastest point of sailing, it is obvious that reaching must be faster than beating, when you will be bashing away against the wind. It may seem surprising that it is also faster than running, when you have the wind right behind you, but the reasons are simple enough. On a run, it is hard to get full value from the sail or sails in front of the mast, because of the blanketing effect of the mainsail. Also, when reaching, there is sideways pressure of the wind to steady the boat, so it is much easier to steer a straight course.

Beating

If a boat is pointed directly into the wind, the sails will only catch the wind when sheeted or pushed out, so that the wind blows on their forward rather than their after surfaces. This means the thrust of the wind will be in the opposite direction from what it should be, and the boat will go backwards.

No boat, therefore, can sail directly against the wind. Even the best-designed sailing craft can do no more than sail as nearly in that direction as possible. In order for the wind to fill the sails, they will have to be sheeted in closer than for reaching. This is why a boat on a beat is said to be *close-hauled*.

A common beginners' mistake is to try to sail too close to the wind; in other words, too directly towards where the wind is coming from. This means the sails will have to be sheeted in too close for them to catch the wind properly. The boat will sail slowly, sluggishly, and may lose the wind altogether, whereupon she may stop sailing altogether and, since the rudder is only effective when the boat is moving through the water, she will not be under control until you get her going again.

Try this experiment when you get the chance. Head the boat too close to the wind. Sheet the sails in too close. She will slow down and go 'dead' in the water. You will feel that she is not

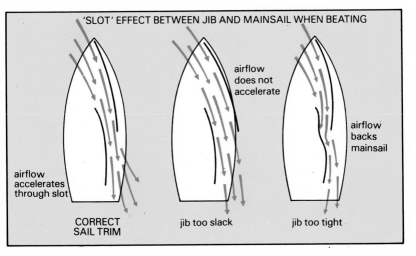

'SLOT' EFFECT BETWEEN JIB AND MAINSAIL WHEN BEATING

airflow does not accelerate

airflow backs mainsail

airflow accelerates through slot

CORRECT SAIL TRIM

jib too slack

jib too tight

under proper control. Now head her off the wind a little and ease the sheets. The boat will almost instantly 'come alive' and pick up speed.

Beating is always a compromise between course and speed, and this compromise will depend on the conditions prevailing at the time – on how strong the wind is, whether there is a tide or current, and if so in which direction, whether your boat is a good performer to windward, and so on. In sailing, no two situations are ever quite the same, which is one of the things that make the whole sport so fascinating.

Left: Going about. The crew are preparing to duck under the boom as it swings across.

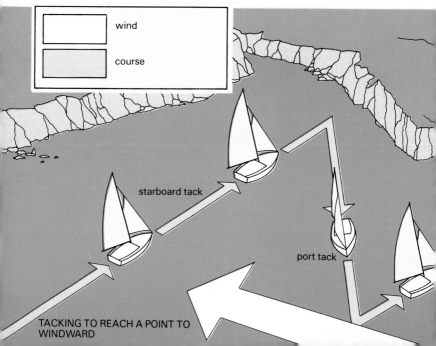

| | wind |
| | course |

starboard tack

port tack

TACKING TO REACH A POINT TO WINDWARD

Tacking

A boat can reach a point directly up to windward by beating first to one side of the objective, then the other – in other words by sailing a zig-zag course. This is known as tacking.

Tacking obviously involves one or more alterations of course, and there is a definite drill for this. The helmsman takes charge of the manoeuvre and gives the necessary orders, of which there are two. The first is *Ready about!'* Changing course from one tack to the other is called 'going about', so this first order means 'Get ready to go about on to the other tack.' The second order is *'Lee-oh!'*, which means he or she is going to push the tiller over to the lee side of the boat, that is, the side opposite that from where the wind is coming.

Thus, 'Ready about' is the warning and 'Lee-oh!' the command. As he or she gives the latter, the helmsman pushes the tiller firmly over to bring the boat round so that the wind is blowing from the other side of her. As the boat alters course into the wind and the jib starts to 'back' (fill with wind from the other side; this helps to take the boat's head round), the crew will release the secured jib sheet and tighten up the slack sheet on the other side (sheet it across). The mainsail will swing across the boat of its own accord, and will be adjusted, if necessary, by the helmsman or another member of the crew.

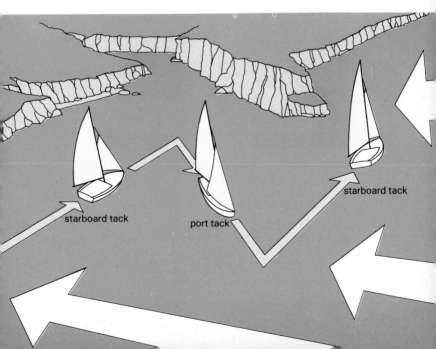

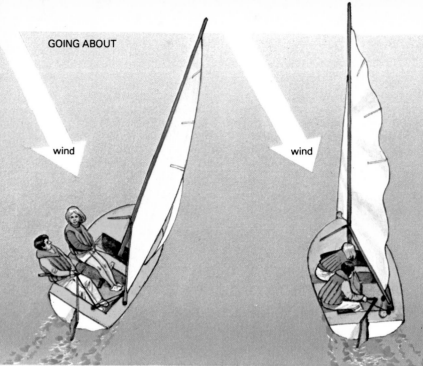

wind

wind

1. Ready about – make sure that the boat is moving fast enough through the water for the rudder to be really effective.

2. Lee-oh – tiller is pushed over to bring the boat round so that the wind will be blowing from the other side of her. Jib sheets should be released and the crew get ready to change sides.

In a small boat such as a dinghy, the crew will also move across to the new windward side, to counteract the heel of the boat on the new tack.

The two tacks have names. When the wind is coming from the starboard side of the boat, she is on the starboard tack. When it is coming from the port side, she is on the port tack. It is of the greatest importance which tack you are on when you are in the vicinity of other vessels, as described later.

There are also some vital rules when going about from one tack to the other.

Firstly, the boat must be moving fast enough through the water for the rudder to be really effective.

Secondly, the helmsman must put the tiller over firmly and decisively so that the boat makes an equally decisive turn across the wind.

If either of these conditions is not met, the boat may merely turn to face the wind and stay there with her sails

wind

wind

3. Sails flap as the jib starts to back and the boat's head swings round. Crew should move to the other side of the boat and tighten up the slack jib sheet on that side.

4. Boom and mainsail swing across of their own accord, and should require little adjustment.

apping and her rudder useless. This called being 'in stays', or 'in irons', nd it is a situation that can be both mbarrassing and dangerous if there re other boats around. The helms- man will have demonstrated his or er inefficiency, and since the boat ill be out of control until she can be ot moving again, she may be a col- sion hazard, especially in a race.

Thirdly, the helmsman must give rders loudly and clearly, so that here is no possibility of their not being heard and understood.

Fourthly, the crew must obey those orders promptly and efficiently. They must be going about, not messing about!

Tacking up to a point directly to windward can be a tedious process, and also a wet one, if there is spray coming over the bows. But it can be the most satisfying part of sailing, too. It means you can get anywhere you want, whichever way the wind may be blowing.

Sail trimming

This means adjusting the sails to the wind at exactly the right angle. So far we have talked about sheeting the sails in too close, or not close enough, and the extremes of these situations will be obvious enough. But how do you tell what is 'just right'?

On a run, with the wind behind you, it does not matter too much. You will have the mainsail set square to the wind, and you will be more concerned with 'winging out' the jib on the other side of the boat or getting the spinnaker to draw properly than anything else.

Dinghies running 'goosewinged', with both jib and spinnaker up.

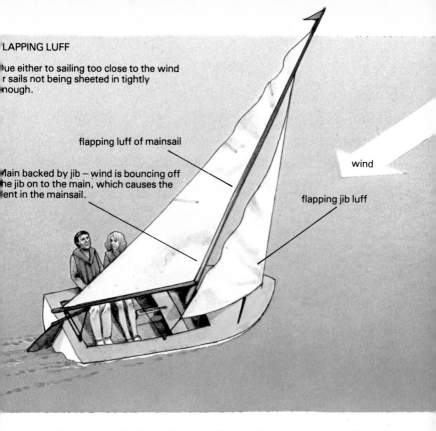

LAPPING LUFF

Due either to sailing too close to the wind
or sails not being sheeted in tightly
enough.

flapping luff of mainsail

Main backed by jib – wind is bouncing off
the jib on to the main, which causes the
dent in the mainsail.

wind

flapping jib luff

On a reach or a beat, the 'set' of the working sails will matter a good deal more. You will know if they are not sheeted in close enough, because the wind won't fill them properly. But how can you tell if they are in *too* close? There they are, as smooth as can be. But somehow the boat feels as though she has got her brakes on.

The mainsail is the clue. You will notice a good helmsman glancing aloft from time to time. Is he looking at the flag at the top of the mast, to check the direction of the wind?

He may be, although he will probably have a pretty good idea where the wind is coming from anyway. He is most likely to be looking at the top of the luff of the mainsail, the area near the top of the mast. This part of the sail should be only gently pressed by the wind, in which case it will 'lift' now and then. If the luff is pressed hard, the sail has been sheeted in too close for the course the boat is on and should be let out a little, which will make her 'easier' and increase her speed. Trim the jib similarly.

65

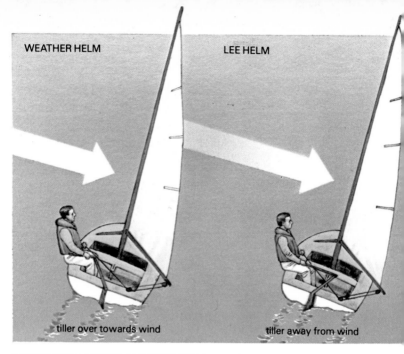

WEATHER HELM

LEE HELM

tiller over towards wind

tiller away from wind

Weather helm

To keep a well-balanced boat on a straight course, one should *have* to hold the tiller a little over towards the side of the boat the wind is coming from (or, with wheel steering, hold the wheel a little the other way). It may seem odd that you should not keep the tiller or the wheel in a central position, but there is a definite and very important reason for it.

It is actually a safety-measure because the boat's sail plan should be balanced in such a way that, left to her own devices, she will turn into the wind. And this means that if the helmsman lets go of the wheel, either accidentally, in an emergency, or even intentionally to tend briefly to something else, the boat will 'heat up' until she is pointing into the wind which will cease to fill the sails. She will stop sailing and just lie there maybe swooping this way and that in short bursts, with a good deal of flapping and banging, but, in normal conditions, in no danger.

A boat which behaves like this is said to carry weather helm. In other words, left to herself, she will turn up into the weather.

The amount of weather helm should be slight, especially if the boat is a big one. If the degree of weather helm is more than slight, the helmsman will constantly have to counter

sheets eased

which will still fill her sails, which means she will continue to sail but will not be under control. In this situation the mainsail is likely to gybe, as a result of which, depending on the force of the wind, the boat may suffer damage to her gear, be dismasted, or even capsize or swamp.

Lee helm has the added disadvantage that, if there is a large degree of it, the boat will be just as difficult and tiring to steer as one with an equivalent degree of weather helm. The only difference is that you are constantly having to stop her turning away from the wind instead of towards it.

Weather helm, then, is a safety factor, enabling wind to be spilled from the sails. There is another way of spilling the wind from a boat's sails when she is too hard-pressed, and that is by easing the sheets, or, if necessary, letting them go completely. The mainsail, being the larger sail, is the one that really matters, so in dinghies, which may capsize without too much warning, the mainsheet should never be made fast but held in the hand so that it can be instantly let go.

Always tie a knot in the end of both your jib sheets and your mainsheet, so that, if you do have to let them fly, they will not run out through their fairleads or blocks and go streaming away on the wind out of your reach.

The best knot for this purpose is the figure-of-eight. It is a very simple knot, and you can see how to make it on page 201.

ct a strong tendency to turn up into he wind. Steering a boat in such ircumstances with a tiller can be ery tiring indeed. Because of the mechanism involved, it will be less iring in the case of a boat with wheel teering, but too much weather helm s still to be avoided since the constant nd excessive angling of the rudder to ne side will reduce the vessel's speed.

Some boats – luckily there are not oo many of them around – will only eep a straight course if the tiller is eld over to the side of the boat *away* rom the wind. This is the lee side, so uch boats are said to carry lee helm. ee helm is most undesirable in that, f the tiller is let go, the boat will turn ot towards but away from the wind

Leeway

This is another factor which has to be taken into consideration when sailing in any direction other than with the wind astern.

Although a sailing boat has a deep keel to prevent it being pushed sideways by the wind, it is impossible for the keel to counter this sideways movement completely. When running, with the wind coming from astern, there is no force in a sideways direction, but when reaching or beating, with the wind coming from the side or ahead, every boat will move not only forward but sideways.

This sideways movement is called leeway, because it is made toward the *lee*, that is, away from the wind.

Leeway is an important aspect of sailing, and allowing for it may call for a good deal of calculation involving the boat's course relative to the wind, how good a performer the boat is on a reach or a beat, whether there is any tide or current running and in which direction, and so on. Suppose there is a buoy ahead which you have

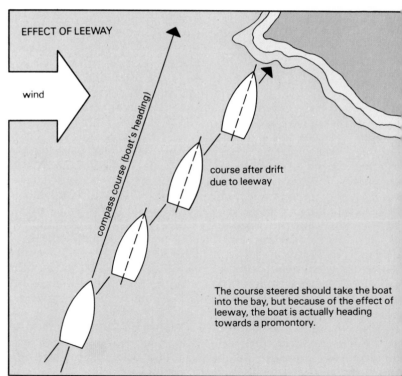

EFFECT OF LEEWAY

wind

compass course (boat's heading)

course after drift
due to leeway

The course steered should take the boat into the bay, but because of the effect of leeway, the boat is actually heading towards a promontory.

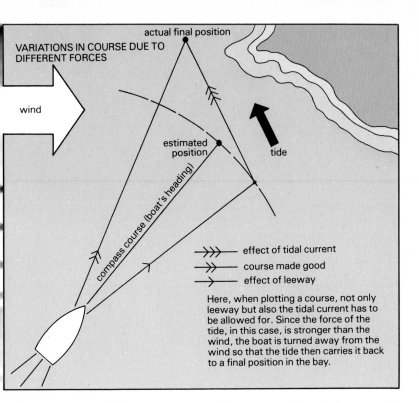

VARIATIONS IN COURSE DUE TO
DIFFERENT FORCES

wind

actual final position

estimated
position

tide

compass course (boat's heading)

>>> — effect of tidal current
>> — course made good
> — effect of leeway

Here, when plotting a course, not only
leeway but also the tidal current has to
be allowed for. Since the force of the
tide, in this case, is stronger than the
wind, the boat is turned away from the
wind so that the tide then carries it back
to a final position in the bay.

to leave to port, which means you must pass to starboard of it. You may say to yourself, 'I've got to allow for leeway. I'm heading straight for the buoy now, in fact a little to starboard of it, but the wind is blowing from starboard. So if I keep on like this, by the time I get there, I'll be on the port side of it, so I'd better do something about it.' On a reach this may be merely a matter of altering course closer to the wind, but if the boat is already on a beat, sailing as close to the wind as she can manage, you will have to tack to get up to windward.

But suppose there is a strong tide running against the wind? This will push the boat up towards the wind, reducing or cancelling out leeway, in which case you can sail directly on to your objective. If the force of the tidal current is greater than that of the wind, you may have to turn away from the wind instead of towards it.

Leeway is another aspect of sailing in which conditions are rarely the same twice over. Allowing for it is, like so many of the skills that go to make up the good small-boat sailor, largely a matter of experience.

First Trip

Once you know something about the theory of sailing, you can put that theory into practice by actually getting afloat.

Getting ready

Suppose you are going out in the sort of boat already described in some detail, namely a sloop-rigged dinghy.

First of all, there is something you must all take with you – a lifejacket. Most sailing clubs make it a rule that anyone who goes out in a dinghy must wear a lifejacket, and this should be observed by everyone, whether they belong to a club or not. Dinghies can capsize. Someone may fall overboard. All sorts of things can happen. **Dinghy sailors should put on their lifejackets before they go aboard, and not take them off until they are ashore again.**

The next thing to do is launch the boat, if she's ashore, or get aboard her if she's afloat.

If you have to launch the boat, you must do so with the keel either in the retracted position, if it is a centre-board, or completely removed, if it is a dagger board.

It may be more convenient to get the sails ready before launching the boat, but it depends on circumstances. You will probably have to bend on the sails, but that has already been described. You may also be able to hoist the sails while the boat is still on dry land.

Dinghies being prepared for launching. All equipment should be checked first.

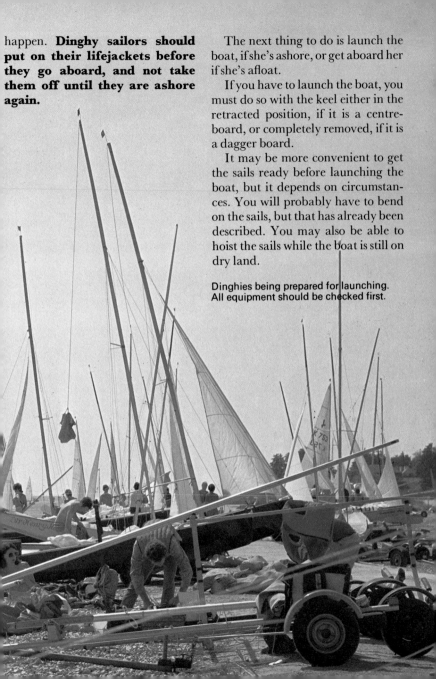

When putting up the sails, it is essential to have the boat facing the wind, or at any rate at such an angle that the sails will not catch the wind before you want them to. If they do, the boat will try to start sailing, and that, whether you're afloat or still ashore, can lead to all sorts of trouble.

If you are afloat, and there are no complications of tide or current to consider, you should always hoist the mainsail first. This will act like the tail of a weather-vane which will keep the boat pointing quietly towards the wind. If you are hoisting the sails before launching, the boat must be pointing in such a direction that the mainsail, with the mainsheet slacked right off, will not catch the wind.

Below: Pupils at Bosham Sea School, England, get a lesson in the importance of having a taut luff.

Involuntary sailing on dry land can be even more disastrous than the same thing on the water.

One important point to note: when hoisting both the jib and the mainsail, you must get the luff as taut as you possibly can, because the 'sharpness' of these leading edges will materially affect the boat's performance, especially to windward; so much so that, if you are racing, it can make all the difference as to whether or not you win.

Getting under way

Now the sails are up, and if the boat was ashore, she has been launched. She is at anchor, on a mooring, attached to a ring or some other securing point on a jetty, or one of the

The crew of this Topper class dinghy have slacked the sail right off, otherwise the boat might take off!

crew may be standing in the water holding her by the bow, waiting to climb aboard as she starts sailing. Whatever her situation, she is afloat, with her bows pointing towards the wind, her sails flapping and her boom swinging from side to side, as though she is impatient to be off. The procedure of starting off is called getting under way.

If the boat has been launched from the shore, first the rudder and tiller must be shipped. This is normally a simple enough business. The forward edge of the rudder has two vertical pins, called *pintles*, which slip into eyelets on the stern of the boat called *gudgeons*.

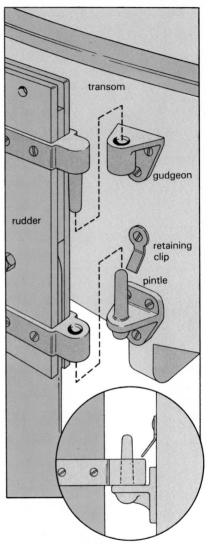

Above: Typical pintle and gudgeon arrangement on a dinghy. Inset shows the retaining clips in the fixed position.

You now have to decide which way you are going to start off, though it may be that you have no choice, because there is open water only to one side. Suppose it is on the left-hand side (see diagram). That means you must head the boat in that direction, which will bring the wind on to your right or starboard side, so you will be getting under way on the starboard tack.

How do you point the bows in the right direction before you have started sailing? There are various methods. To start with, whichever method you choose, you must sheet in the sails fairly close, so that the wind will soon fill them. Then, if there is any tide or current running in the same direction as the wind, you can put the tiller over to starboard to turn the boat's bows the way you want to go. If you are on a mooring, the crew member casting off (letting go) at the bow can also give a pull ahead, which can give the boat a sheer the right way. The same can be done when casting off from a jetty or pier.

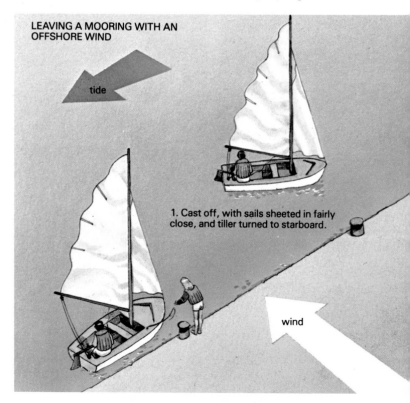

LEAVING A MOORING WITH AN OFFSHORE WIND

tide

1. Cast off, with sails sheeted in fairly close, and tiller turned to starboard.

wind

74

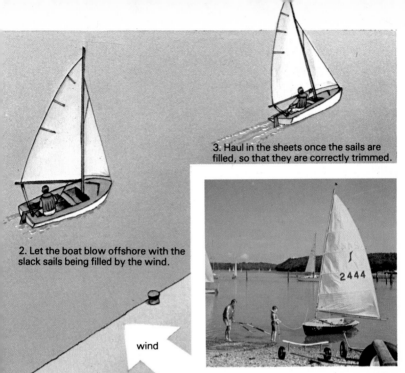

3. Haul in the sheets once the sails are filled, so that they are correctly trimmed.

2. Let the boat blow offshore with the slack sails being filled by the wind.

wind

Above: A dinghy safely held to windward.

A small, but important, point here: when making fast to anything ashore, you should always take a line from your boat, through or round the ring, bollard, or whatever it is you are securing to, and back to the boat again. Then, when the time comes to cast off, you can let go the line on board and pull it in through the ring or round the bollard, instead of having to scramble ashore to untie a knot and either doing a 'pierhead jump' or getting left behind altogether when the boat sails away.

Another method of getting the boat to point in the right direction is to sheet the jib out on the opposite side of the boat to that in which you want to go, so that the wind will blow the bows round. Simplest of all, the member of the crew standing in the water can push the boat round until she is heading the right way.

Before you get under way, or as soon as you reach deep enough water, lower the centreboard to stop sideways drift. With open water on the left and the wind on your right, you will have to start off on a beat, close-hauled on the starboard tack. Open water will give you a chance to settle down and get the feel of the boat.

Keeping to the course

In the distance, fine on the port bow – in other words, just slightly to the left of the way you are heading – the shoreline sticks out in a small promontory, then falls away again. Once you are past that point, you will really be in open water. For a while it may seem as if you are going to get past the projecting spit of land all right. Your bows are still pointing at clear water beyond the end of it.

But gradually leeway takes its toll. You must remember that all the time the boat is moving ahead, she is 'crabbing' sideways as well. This will be borne in on you when you discover that, although you have not altered course, your bows are pointing first at the end of the land, and then some distance inshore of the end.

Your instinct may be to head the

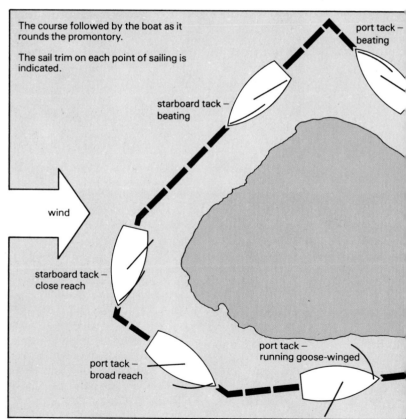

The course followed by the boat as it rounds the promontory.

The sail trim on each point of sailing is indicated.

port tack – beating

starboard tack – beating

wind

starboard tack – close reach

port tack – broad reach

port tack – running goose-winged

boat a little more out from the shore, more in the direction the wind is coming from. But suppose you can't do that because you are already sailing as close to the wind as you can? If you tried, the sails would no longer draw properly. The boat would slow down, make more leeway than she is doing, and you would probably end up still further inshore.

The only thing to do is to tack, in other words, turn to starboard until the wind is coming over the port instead of the starboard bow. You will then be heading out from the shore. You can stay on this tack – the port tack, because the wind is now coming from the port side – until you are far enough out to turn back on to the starboard tack again.

When you do this, you should find that you are far enough out to 'weather' the promontory with ease. (To 'weather' something means to get past it on the side the weather, that is, the wind, is coming from.)

Beyond the promontory, the shoreline bends away in a long curve. When you follow it round, the wind will 'draw aft', which means it blows from further and further astern, so you can let both the mainsail and the jib out further and further. As the land continues to curve away, the beat you were on to start with will become a close reach, a reach, a broad reach, and perhaps a run.

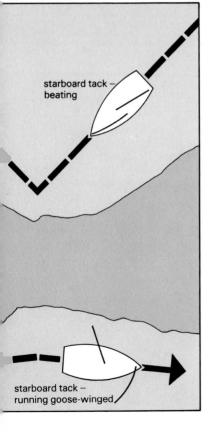

starboard tack –
beating

starboard tack –
running goose-winged

Return trip

Imagine you have turned so far off the wind now that you are running, with the mainsail out to port, at right-angles to the centreline of the boat. The wind is coming from astern, just a little on the starboard side.

If you turn off the wind any more, you will bring the wind on to the port quarter. In other words, it will be blowing from astern on the port side. The wind will then be on the same side as the mainsail, which means you will be sailing by the lee, and therefore liable to gybe.

You started on a beat which became a reach and then a run, so you have been on all the points of sailing, and perhaps it is time to turn back.

The question is, which way to turn? If you decide to go round to port, you will bring the wind forward on the same side of the boat as the mainsail until it blows on the forward or 'wrong' side of the sail, causing it to swing across the boat, or in other words, gybe.

Gybing is a perfectly legitimate manoeuvre. But experience is needed to do it properly, so, since this your first trip, turn towards the wind instead, to starboard. This will bring you successively on to a broad reach, a reach, a close reach, and then a beat on the starboard tack; in fact the reverse of the points of sailing you went through when you were 'outward bound'.

You should have no trouble with the promontory on the way back, because by then you will have the wind behind you again, which means there won't be any narrow limit to the course you can take. In fact, once you are running again, it should be 'plain sailing' back to the beach or jetty or mooring buoy or wherever you started from.

Approaching a mooring

The most difficult parts of sailing are getting under way and picking up a mooring or coming alongside. A sailing boat needs to approach its terminal point as slowly as possible, consistent with safety. This is done by coming in against the wind.

How a boat approaches her terminal point will depend on her point of sailing in the early stages of the approach. If the wind is coming from ahead, it will be simply a question of beating or tacking up to her objective. If the wind is coming from the side, she may approach on a reach and turn up into the wind at a point

APPROACHING A MOORING

Approach on a reach. Turn up into the wind at a point from which the boat can fetch the rest of the way.

which will allow her to 'fetch' the rest of the way, which means her momentum through the water will get her there. This is a comparatively easy procedure when coming in to a beach or alongside a jetty, but a lot harder when you have to pick up an isolated buoy, in which case it may be better to sail past the mooring, then turn and tack back to it.

There remains the question of what to do when you have the wind astern in the initial stages of the approach. This depends on what you are coming in to. If it is a buoy, you may decide to sail past and beat or tack back. If it is a beach or a jetty, you can turn into the wind some time before you get there, lower the mainsail, then cover the remaining distance under jib alone, which can be slacked off or let fly in the final stages. This procedure can, of course, also be used when coming in to a mooring.

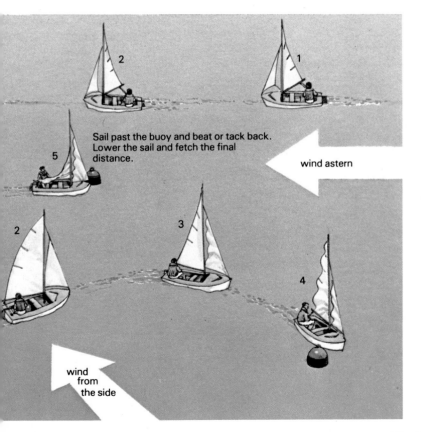

Sail past the buoy and beat or tack back. Lower the sail and fetch the final distance.

wind astern

wind from the side

The one thing you must make sure of is that, when you finally arrive, neither of your sails is still catching the wind.

Handing sails

Lowering sails is known as handing them. This should preferably be done with the boat lying head to wind. The sail or sails will then come down *inboard,* within the limits of the boat. It may sometimes be necessary to hand sails with the wind coming from the beam, and in that case they will be blowing out at right-angles to the boat, so will be more trouble to get down.

The jib may be lowered with the wind coming from astern, but this may be difficult as the wind will still try to fill it as it comes down. The mainsail should never be lowered when the wind is astern, except in very light airs.

When handing sails, the one nearest the bow should be lowered first, then the next aft – and the next, if there is a 'next', as there may be in the case of two-masted rigs. This means that, if the boat is afloat, she will, throughout the sail-handing procedure, act as a weather-vane.

On larger boats it is usual to leave the mainsail neatly folded down on the boom, preferably with a sail cover to protect it. If it is a cabin boat, the jib will probably be stowed below. In the case of dinghies, it is customary to remove the sails completely at the end of an outing.

On larger boats, the mainsail is usually left furled along the boom, with a special cover to protect it.

Racing

Most people begin their sailing careers in dinghies, which is an excellent way to start off. In a number of important respects. a dinghy demands more of her crew than does a larger boat. It is natural to think that the smaller a boat is, the easier she will be to sail, but this is not true. Everything will happen more slowly aboard a larger boat. She will heel over more slowly, and she is unlikely to capsize. If you make a mistake, she will probably just lie there, maybe protesting a bit with her sails and gear, waiting for you to sort it out, whereas, if you made the same mistake in a dinghy, you might well be in the water.

In a dinghy, if there is much breeze, you have to concentrate on balancing the boat, the trim of the sails, going about, and every touch on the tiller. It is not surprising that the crews of the big ocean racers are largely recruited from dinghy sailors, and that good dinghy helmsmen are especially in demand for these larger boats.

Most dinghy sailors spend much of their time racing. This is usually because there is a limit to how much pleasure and satisfaction you can get out of messing around in a small open boat in a restricted area. If you race, the sport takes on an added dimension. You not only have to do your

The line-up for the start of a race. The trick is to be on the line at the 'off'. This should be an exciting start.

best against the wind and water; you find yourself in competition with other dinghy sailors as well. You will take a new interest in improving both your boat's performance and your own.

Good dinghy racing demands skilled helmsmanship and highly efficient sail-handling, plus an expert knowledge of tactics and the rules of the game (see page 88). The fact that it is a highly-regarded Olympic sport indicates what an important aspect of the sailing scene dinghy racing is.

Most clubs which sail dinghies specialize in one class of boat, or there may be one class for the seniors and another for the junior members. In addition there will almost certainly be an assortment of other boats around as well.

Of course all sorts of boats can race against each other, and their crews may well get a lot of fun out of doing so. The only trouble is that such races are not a true test of skill since the boats themselves will differ in performance. Allowances may be made for this by handicapping, but it is a difficult thing to do accurately, and is rarely undertaken with dinghies.

The idea behind class racing is that, since all the boats competing will be the same in all important respects, it will be the best crew and not the best boat that wins (although the maintenance of the boat may play a material part). This greatly increases the sense of competition, and brings out a higher degree of skill on the part of the competitors.

Racing classes

Boats fall into various classes or categories, depending on how rigid the class rules are.

Formula class
These boats are allowed to differ a little in the shape of their hulls, the size of their sails, and what sort of equipment they have. What matters is that when these various factors are expressed mathematically, all the boats will have the same performance potential. This may sound – and is – all very technical, but the basic idea of allowing some variation of shape, sail area and so on, is to permit a degree of experiment, either on an amateur level by the owners of these boats themselves, or by professional boat-builders.

Below: Boats of the 5·5 metre category, formula class, tacking to windward as they race.

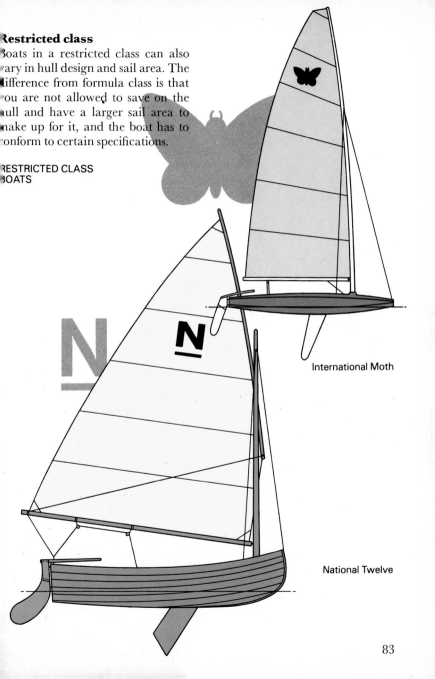

Restricted class

Boats in a restricted class can also vary in hull design and sail area. The difference from formula class is that you are not allowed to save on the hull and have a larger sail area to make up for it, and the boat has to conform to certain specifications.

RESTRICTED CLASS
BOATS

International Moth

National Twelve

83

One-design class

These boats are the most 'alike' of all. Only very minor differences are allowed.

Both restricted and one-design classes may be governed by other rules as well, for example, how often the sails may be renewed, or how often you may paint the hull, or scrub the boat's bottom. Restrictions of this kind are intended to prevent those dinghy owners who have the most time and money gaining an advantage over others less fortunate.

You will find a selection of popular sailing dinghies of various classes in the last chapter.

ONE-DESIGN CLASS BOATS

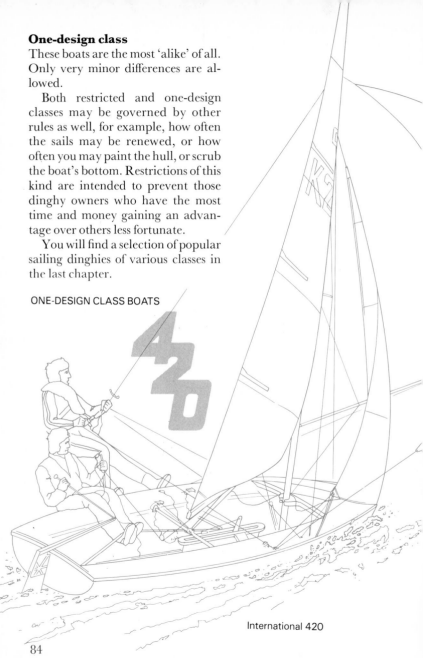

International 420

International Finn

National Firefly

Mirror

Tasar

ONE-DESIGN
CLASS BOATS

International Cadet

International Fireball

86

International Dragon

International 5-0-5

International 470

87

Racing rules and tactics

The start

A race starts when, on a given signal, the competing boats cross the starting line. This is an imaginary line, usually between a point on shore (probably the clubhouse, if there is one), and a stationary boat, or buoy, or some other sighting mark at the other end of the line.

Before the start, the boats manoeuvre for position with a three-fold aim; firstly, to be on the line at the starting signal; secondly, to be sailing as fast as possible at that moment; and, thirdly, to be far enough clear of the other competing boats for their sails not to *take their wind* (blanket them, as the mainsail blankets the jib on a run).

The race may be started by a flag signal, or a gun, or both. If it is being started by a gun, look for the smoke of it firing instead of listening for the report. Vision is quicker than hearing, and you should be able to get away that second or so sooner that may make all the difference.

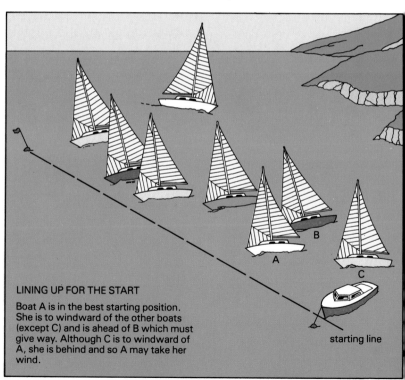

LINING UP FOR THE START

Boat A is in the best starting position. She is to windward of the other boats (except C) and is ahead of B which must give way. Although C is to windward of A, she is behind and so A may take her wind.

starting line

Mid-race tactics

You must follow the best course you can to the first racing buoy or whatever mark it is you have to sail round, making the most of the wind (including doing your best to prevent anybody else taking it), and allowing for any tide or current there may be.

You should also aim to come up to the mark with the wind on the starboard side (on the starboard tack). There are 'rules of the road' afloat just as there are on land (see page 133), and one of these is that a boat on the starboard tack has the right of way over one on the port tack (with the wind on the port side). This means that, if a boat on the starboard tack and one on the port tack are dead-heating at a mark, the one on

Rounding a marker buoy. Note that all the boats are on the starboard tack. Those down-wind are still close-hauled. The leaders are running.

the port tack will have to give way.

Most races involve the three points of sailing, namely beating, reaching and running. The tactics described so far mainly apply to beating and reaching. When running, your main tactic should be to keep your own wind clear and at the same time, if possible, blanket the boat ahead.

The finish

When coming up to the finishing line, try to cross it at the nearest and most favourable point, which will probably be as nearly as possible at right-angles to it.

Racing in larger boats

Needless to say, racing is very much a part of the bigger-boat scene as well. Here, however, class racing is much less common, since the larger craft owned by members of any one club are likely to be much more varied. Most of these races are therefore organized on a handicap basis.

The same racing rules apply as for dinghies, in theory anyway, but won't be applied so frequently. Because of differences in perform-ance, and the fact that the course will probably be longer, two or more boats are much less likely to find themselves so often in close proximity as would be the case in a dinghy race. The starboard tack rule, for instance, is less important, except at the start, and situations in which you can take another boat's wind will not occur very often, except, again, at the start. On a long race, you may not even see any of the other competitors for hours on end!

Bigger-boat racing can be any-thing from a local club affair to ocean-going racing. Both have the same basic satisfactions as dinghy racing, namely of doing your best against the wind and water, and a bit better than somebody else as well.

The foregoing is, of course, only

the most elementary introduction to racing. Once the racing 'bug' has bitten you, as it probably will, you would do well to acquaint yourself with the current racing rules of the Royal Yachting Association (or its equivalent outside the United Kingdom) as soon and as thoroughly as you can. The rest is experience – with a bit of natural talent thrown in.

A wonderful sight – racing yachts with their spinnakers up, taking advantage of a fresh breeze.

Cruising

Essentially, cruising is making a trip somewhere, and living on board at least overnight. It may be a modest venture to the next creek up the coast, or a voyage round the world.

Cruising is not quite so easy to take up as the type of sailing discussed so

A boom tent like the one pictured here can provide sleeping accommodation, and shelter during the day as well.

far. One problem is that there are not so many places where you can do it.

It is easier now than it was a few years ago. This is because of the welcome appearance of a number of small cruising boats that can be trailed behind a car. Cruising also tends to be a more expensive type of sailing, although it does not have to be. It depends on how much discomfort you are prepared to put up with.

What kind of boat can you go cruising in? The answer is, almost anything, provided there is room in the bottom for you to stretch out. If it is a dinghy, it will help if she is half-decked (decked-in at the bows) to provide dry stowage for your bedding and other gear. At night you turn the boat into a tent by rigging a water-proof sheet over the boom and attaching it to the sides of the boat. You can either lie at anchor or pick up a mooring if there is one available.

This type of sailing is generally known as *camping-cruising*, and it can be great fun. Naturally, it has its limitations. If you want to go in for cruising, it should be possible. In a cruising area, you may be able to join a club (you don't have to own a boat to do that), and then you ought to be able to get a crewing job now and again, especially as you become more experienced. Finally, you can go on one of the cruising holidays offered by youth organizations, sailing schools, and commercial charter firms.

Equipment

A modern cruising sloop which could be used for offshore racing, too. Note her wide beam.

First of all, you need a suitable boat. Secondly, since you are going to live aboard, you need some sort of protection from the weather. As already described, a large dinghy with a tent over the boom will do, but a proper cabin boat will obviously be a lot better. Thirdly, if you are going to stay aboard for long, you will need some means of cooking. This will probably be a paraffin or gas stove.

Many boats which cruise on inland waters have masts which can be lowered for passing under bridges, and cabin tops which you can raise when the boat is not sailing, to give more *headroom* (more room to stand up). Generally speaking, such boats need not be so robustly built as those which sail on the sea. A lifting cabin-top, for example, would be a definite hazard at sea, since a wave sweeping the boat could lift it and fill the cabin below. But all boats, whether sea-going or not, should be 'well-found', which means not only that the boat should be properly designed, well-built, and sound, but also that her spars, rigging, sails, steering gear and so on work efficiently and are adequate for any conditions she is likely to encounter.

There is a world of difference between sailing on inland waters and on the open sea. The latter can be really rugged, and calls for a good deal of experience. Most sailing folk come to it, if they come to it at all, after serving an apprenticeship sailing in comparatively sheltered waters such as estuaries, the tidal reaches of rivers,

This Volvo diesel engine has the twin advantages of power and reliability. It must be kept in good working order.

protected bays, stretches between the mainland and an island or islands comparatively close off-shore, and so on. Sailing in these areas, you can poke your bows out to sea now and again, and gradually get used to the 'real thing.'

There is one other thing that ought to be specifically mentioned. Although the boat is primarily a sailing craft, she may have an engine. If so, it *must* be kept in good working order. A lot of sailing people think it is a slight on their skill to have an engine to rely on in an emergency, so they tend to ignore it until that emergency comes along – and then it will not work. To have an engine that will not work when you want it to is worse than not having one at all.

Cruising boats

A mini-cruiser. Boats like this one are roomier than predecessors of the same size, and are easy to trail behind a car and launch.

Conventional, heavy-keeled boats are classified by their *tonnage* (a British system of boat measurement widely used). At the bottom of this classification comes the two-and-a-half ton boat, which will be about 5·5 metres long, no longer than a big dinghy.

This is about the smallest cabin boat it is practicable to live aboard. Older boats of this size will accommodate two people but they will find themselves cramped. There will only be sitting headroom. In other words, people will be able to sit up straight, but not stand up. Five ton boats are more likely to have standing head-

room, but then it may only be in the main cabin, or at the after end of the main cabin, where there may be more height than there is further forward. When this raised area of the deck structure occurs, it is a permanent part of the cabin top and not adjustable as in the case of the 'inland' boat, and it is called a *doghouse*.

New boats of this size may even have four berths and headroom throughout. Generally speaking, the newer the boat, the roomier she will be. Some very old boats have extremely poor accommodation for their size.

A typical boat

A modern four or five ton boat will probably have four berths, two in the main cabin amidships and two up in the forward part of the boat. The two in the main cabin are usually permanent fixtures and are known as *settee berths* because they are used for sitting as well as sleeping on. There may be fixed berths in the forward cabin too, or they may be *pipe cots*. A pipe cot is simply a rectangle of some kind of canvas-like material stretched over a frame of metal piping – a sort of hammock. The advantage of such berths is that they can be stowed flat against the boat's side when not in use, to give more room up forward, which will make it easier to get at sails or any other items of gear that may be stowed in the bows.

In many respects a five-tonner is an ideal size for anyone without a great deal of experience. Such a boat will be stable and big enough to 'forgive' your mistakes, but not too big to handle easily.

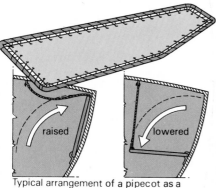

Typical arrangement of a pipecot as a forecabin berth.

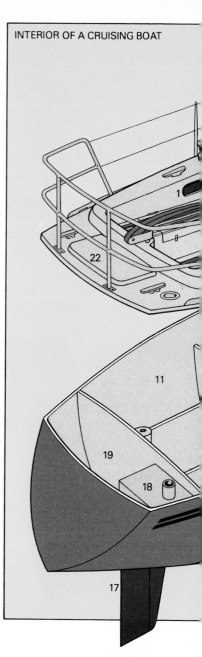

INTERIOR OF A CRUISING BOAT

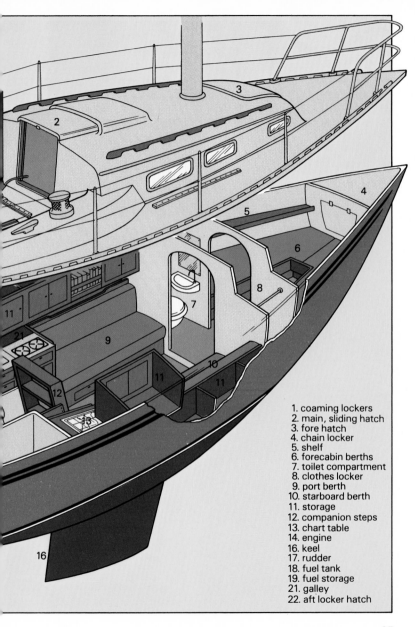

1. coaming lockers
2. main, sliding hatch
3. fore hatch
4. chain locker
5. shelf
6. forecabin berths
7. toilet compartment
8. clothes locker
9. port berth
10. starboard berth
11. storage
12. companion steps
13. chart table
14. engine
16. keel
17. rudder
18. fuel tank
19. fuel storage
21. galley
22. aft locker hatch

97

Foredeck A typical five-tonner can be divided into three sections, starting from the bows. First there is the foredeck, with the forecabin below. In the forecabin there are two bunks and stowage for sails and other gear. Right up in the bows (this part of the boat is called the *forepeak*) is the anchor chain. When not in use, the anchor is stowed in the foredeck, and its chain is fed down into the forepeak through a metal pipe called a *navel pipe* (some nautical terms are very curious). There may also be a forehatch giving access to the forward part of the boat, and through which sails, for example, can be passed up.

Midships Next is the middle section or midships, the widest part of the boat. There is a cabin-top here, with a doghouse at the after end and a

sliding hatch cover. There are por holes in the cabin top and narro decks on either side.

Below decks is the main cabi where the crew eat and a couple them sleep. (It is traditional, i cidentally, for the skipper to have t starboard-side berth.) A small fol ing table is sited between the tw berths, and at the after-end of t cabin, under the doghouse, is t *galley* (a sea-going kitchen), usual consisting of a cooking stove and bowl inset into a flat surface, f washing up. The stove has two burı ers and uses paraffin or gas.

The stove hangs in a metal fram This is so that it can swing with t movement of the boat and th

Right: Main cabin, looking forward to t forecabin. Note the comfortable settee berths on each side.

Below: Foredeck, with hatch giving access to forecabin below and the sails which are stored in it.

Below: This type of foredeck, made of narrow planks, is called a 'laid' deck. In the foreground, a CQR anchor.

stay level. Anything suspended in this way is said to be in *gymbals*. There are stowages for pots, pans, plates, cutlery and so on around the galley.

The galley may be situated on either the port or starboard side, but often on the port side. The advantage of this is that if any cooking is to be done while under way then it can be done when the boat is on the starboard tack (right of way) with the galley 'downhill' and therefore easier and more comfortable to use. There is less chance of a change of tack during the preparation of a meal if the boat is on the starboard tack and has right of way.

On smaller cruisers, there will not be room for a full-sized navigation table but a flat surface for chart work is required. Therefore, it is usual to have a wooden cover over the washing-up area to be used as a chart table. When plotting a course on a chart, a flat surface on which to lay out the chart is essential because you have to draw lines on it with a ruler.

Everything movable, not only in the main cabin but throughout the boat, must be secured in place and safely stowed away before you set sail. There is nothing more discouraging than to have plates and mugs, books and clothing cascading on to the cabin floor as the boat heels in a strong wind, especially if you are feeling cold and tired and possibly sea sick, too.

Below: A well-equipped galley. The stove is mounted on gymbals so that it will remain level. Good meals are important.

Below: Sea toilet. The toilet will only be enclosed from the rest of the cabin on larger vessels.

Cockpit The third and aftermost section consists mainly of the area from which the boat is controlled. This is known as the cockpit. At the rear will be the helmsman, sitting or standing, usually up to windward. Ahead of him (or her) will be the crew member or members in charge of the jib sheets, one to port and one to starboard. The jib sheets lead from the clew of the sail down either side of the boat, through metal eyes (*fairleads*) to *sheet winches*, one on either side of the cockpit. From the winches the sheets run to securing points, either standard cleats where the sheet can be tied off or *jamming cleats*.

The sheet winch is a fitting, in shape rather like a large cotton reel,

Above: A sheet winch is used to get extra tension. This type, operated by a rotary handle, is called a 'coffee-grinder'.

Below: The cockpit of a large, modern sailing yacht. Note the wheel steering, and the number of winches she has.

Below: View aft of the cockpit of a cruising boat. Her gear may not be glamorous, but it's in good order.

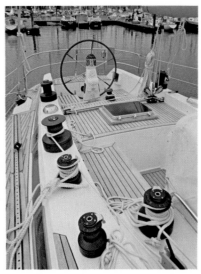

which revolves when operated by a lever. It is prevented by a ratchet mechanism from turning back in the opposite direction. The sheet is wound several times round the drum of the winch, and pulled in by using the lever (or handle). A winch makes it possible to haul the sheet in more easily, in a more controlled fashion, and also 'harder' than can be done by hand alone.

In a small, five-ton cruising boat no space is wasted. There will be lockers or at least open-fronted stowages under the cockpit seats and possibly across the stern as well. This is the place to stow dangerous commodities such as petrol, paraffin, bottled gas, and anything else that won't spoil in the open air. This may include cans of fuel and fresh water, ropes, fenders (sausage-shaped plastic 'bumpers' used to prevent damage when coming alongside another boat or jetty), and even fresh vegetables!

Above: A compact compass-wheel arrangement enabling the helmsman to obtain a good view of the compass card. *Below:* Not a motor cruiser! Some modern yachts have instrument panels monitoring wind velocity, angle of heel, and so on.

Above: Fenders should always be put out to protect a boat's hull when lying alongside a jetty, etc.

Below: A gas locker. No fuel of any kind should be stowed inside the boat. Containers must be secured.

A boat using bottled gas may have the cylinder positioned out in the cockpit with a supply pipe leading in to the stove. In such a case both the cylinder and the supply pipe must be very firmly secured, to guard against any rupturing caused by the movement of the boat, or even by an accidental knock. Bottled gas is fine if proper precautions are taken, but extremely dangerous if they are not.

Some very small boats only have outboard motors which can be easily removed and stowed away, or there may be an inboard engine, usually under the cockpit floor, if there is room. Do remember that a boat's engine must be kept in good working order. They are much more exposed to damp conditions than the engine of a car, and, in a sea-going boat, to the corrosive effects of salt. They need regular inspection and frequent maintenance.

Anchors and anchor work

So far not much has been said about *ground tackle*, as a boat's anchoring equipment is called. Obviously this and its correct use are important elements in sailing.

Types of anchor

Anchors come in various shapes and sizes. The traditional type, the one most people see in their mind's eye as well as on naval cap-badges and so on, is called a *Fisherman's anchor*.

A Fisherman's anchor consists of a straight central member called a shank with a fixed, rigid member or curved crosspiece at the bottom of the shank, with ends which broaden out into spade-like prongs or flukes. At the top of the shank is a movable bar which slides through a hole at the top of the shank. When not in use, the bar lies along the shank, to make the anchor easier to stow. When prepared for use, the bar is pushed half-way through the hole in the shank and secured by a small metal pin or wedge.

The bar passes through the shank at right-angles to the flukes, so that, when the anchor is lowered to the bottom and a pull comes on it, the bar will 'trip' the anchor over one way or the other and cause one of the flukes to dig in.

Nowadays the Fisherman's anchor has been almost completely replaced by a type shaped like the blade of a plough and commonly called a

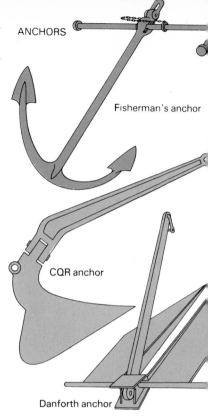

ANCHORS

Fisherman's anchor

CQR anchor

Danforth anchor

'CQR'. The plough blade is hinged where it meets the shank. The CQR has three distinct advantages over the Fisherman's: it has much greater holding power, which means a lighter anchor can be used; with the Fisherman's there will almost always be one exposed fluke, around which the anchor chain may possibly get caught and pull the anchor out – this cannot happen with the CQR, which has no exposed fluke; the CQR is easier and quicker to stow after use because there is no trip-bar to unship.

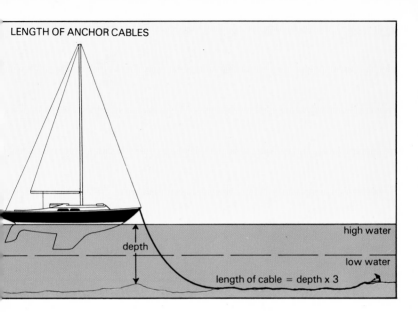

LENGTH OF ANCHOR CABLES

high water

depth

low water

length of cable = depth x 3

Anchor 'cables'

Some small boats use rope instead of chain for their anchor 'cable', but chain is much to be preferred for anything except dinghies. This is not only for reasons of strength and durability, but also because the weight of the chain will cause it to lie along the bottom for some of its length, and its drag along the bottom will be an important addition to the holding-power of the anchor, exerting a more horizontal pull, which will make the anchor more efficient. A horizontal pull will cause it to dig in further, whereas a pull at an angle to the bottom could pull it free.

For the foregoing reasons you should veer (let out) a length of cable considerably more than the depth of water at the anchoring spot, es-

pecially in areas where a strong tide backed up by a strong wind blowing in the same direction may exert a heavy strain on a boat's ground tackle. You must also allow for the fact that a length of cable sufficient to hold your boat at low water may not do so at high water. Taking this and possible weather conditions into consideration, you should make it a rule to veer a length of cable equal to at least three times the depth at high water where you are anchoring.

Your anchor may of course come in useful for purposes other than staying somewhere overnight, or for a longer period. You may want to drop the hook until the tide turns in your favour; or – in an emergency – to stop you drifting on to a lee shore; or perhaps just to go for a swim.

Snugging down

Closely-packed boats snugged down at St. Malo, on France's northern coast. Marinas like this provide safe and easy anchorage.

Having anchored, there is nothing more to be done except 'snug down'. The sails must be lowered and secured. The jib need not be unbent (removed), but it must be prevented from blowing out in the wind. It can be neatly bundled up and tied to some part of the boat, perhaps to the pulpit or a guardrail. The mainsheet must also be hauled in as close as possible, to prevent the boom swinging about.

During the hours of darkness a single white light must be exhibited to indicate your presence, that you are at anchor, and to give some idea of your boat's size. The light may be electric, in which case it will probably be at the masthead; or the more traditional paraffin lamp, which is hoisted on the forestay. This anchor light is called a riding light, because in 'sailorese' a vessel 'rides' at anchor.

However, before you reach this stage of a cruise, you have to decide where you are going and how to get there – you will have to navigate.

Navigation

Navigation involves being informed about the waters you are sailing through, which way you are heading, and just where you are at any given time. Nobody should attempt to go cruising beyond the limits of their navigational ability.

It means finding the way from here to there, avoiding obstacles and getting where you are going as quickly and safely as possible, which are not always the same thing. For example, if you are sailing on the sea and try to take a short cut across a shoal (a shallow area), you may run aground, and, if the tide is falling, you will be left high and dry, and have to spend some considerable time there. If the weather blows up rough before you can get under way again, you could find yourself in a dangerous situation.

Broadly speaking, there are two kinds of navigation, which can be termed 'deep-sea' and 'inshore'. The first is practised when the vessel is out of sight of land. It is based on observations of the position of the sun and other heavenly bodies and so is known as celestial navigation. Nowadays, ocean-going vessels have all sorts of electronic aids to navigation, but the old methods are still employed, if only as a check.

The second kind of navigation is the one more likely to concern us. It is done mainly by observation of visual marks such as buoys and lighthouses.

Well and truly aground – and likely to be there for a long time! Never try to cross shoal waters on a falling tide.

This is sometimes called pilotage, because it is the method employed by pilots when they are 'conning' (directing the course of) a vessel in or out of harbour.

Charts

The first requirement is a chart of the sailing area; perhaps more than one, if you are going some distance, or want to study a particular anchorage.

A chart is a map of an area of water. If any land is shown, it will be only in outline and giving just its major features, especially any prominent landmarks such as church spires or high ground which the sailor may find useful to steer by.

The water area depicted on a chart will be much more detailed, showing safe, deep-water channels; hazards such as rocks and sandbanks; the buoys, lightships and so on which mark these safe passages and dangers; and many other things.

There are two main kinds of chart – those produced officially for commercial purposes, in other words, for shipping, and charts intended specifically for small boat sailors. The official, commercial charts are very accurate, and a lot of yachtsmen prefer them, but they are intended for ships rather than boats, and consequently do not give all the details most of us need to know: such things as the depths of water in creeks and minor rivers, or the location of marinas and yacht anchorages.

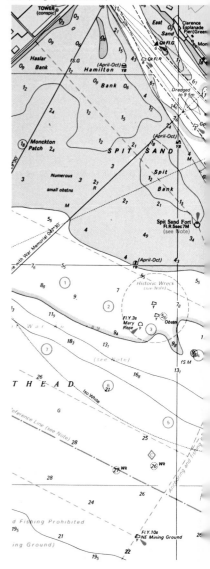

Above: British Admiralty chart of the entrance to Portsmouth Harbour, England.

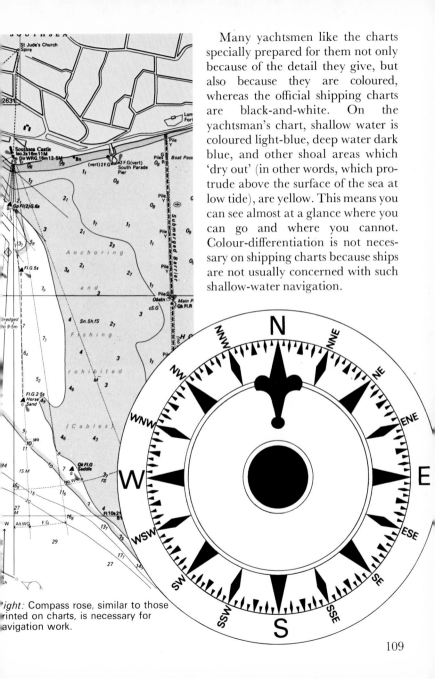

Many yachtsmen like the charts specially prepared for them not only because of the detail they give, but also because they are coloured, whereas the official shipping charts are black-and-white. On the yachtsman's chart, shallow water is coloured light-blue, deep water dark blue, and other shoal areas which 'dry out' (in other words, which protrude above the surface of the sea at low tide), are yellow. This means you can see almost at a glance where you can go and where you cannot. Colour-differentiation is not necessary on shipping charts because ships are not usually concerned with such shallow-water navigation.

Right: Compass rose, similar to those printed on charts, is necessary for navigation work.

In addition to navigational marks such as buoys, charts show obstructions, for example wrecks; prohibited areas which you may not enter, or not at certain times, perhaps because it is a gunnery or bombing range; and areas where you are not allowed to anchor, possibly because there is an oil or gas pipeline along the sea-bed, or a telephone cable.

Here and there on the chart are large circles showing the points of the compass. These are known as *compass roses*, and the purpose of these will be discussed later. There may also be inset 'chartlets' on a larger scale, giving details of harbours and anchorages, just as motoring maps sometimes incorporate 'maplets' of major towns. There may be tabulated information about tides and tidal streams; and, on yachtsmen's charts, there will probably be lines indicating safe courses in the area.

Like maps, charts are drawn to quite a wide range of scales. Distances can be calculated from the scale shown down the sides.

Charts are available from chart agents and most shops which sell nautical gear. When buying them, you must make sure they are up-to-date. If there have been any changes since they were published – if, for example, the position of a buoy has been altered, or anchoring in a particular location prohibited – the charts should have been corrected accordingly. Once they come into your possession, making any further changes will be your responsibility.

TYPICAL CHART WITH DETAILS OF HARBOUR INSET

Particular depths are indicated throughout the chart in metres

SYMBOLS USED

Quality of the bottom

St.	stones
Sh.	shells
G.	gravel
S.	sand
M.	mud

buoy with light – **port** lateral mark

buoy with light – **starboard** lateral ma

red buoy

black buoy

anchorage

cable

wr. wreck

2 drying height

† Ch. Spire church with spire

lighthouse

wreck showing portion of hull

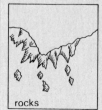

rocks

cliffs

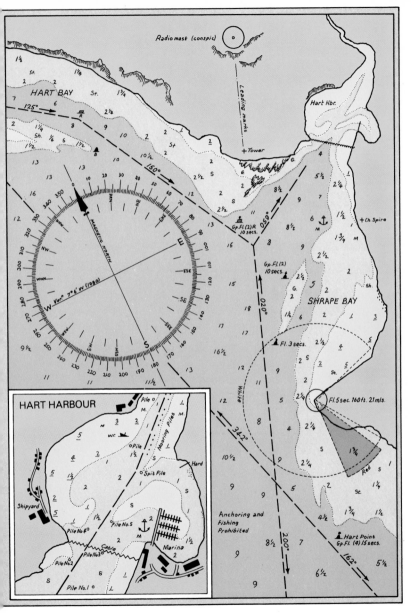

Radio mast (conspic)

Leading marks

HART BAY

HART HARBOUR

Shipyard

Pile No.4
Pile No.3
Pile No.2
Pile No.1

Spit Pile
Pile No.5
Mooring Piles

Marina

Cable

Hard

Wr.

Pile

Hart Hbr.

SHRAPE BAY

Anchoring and
Fishing Prohibited

Gp.Fl.(2)R
10 secs.

Gp.Fl.(2)
10 secs.

Fl. 3 secs.

Fl. 5 sec. 160 ft. 21 mls.

Hart Point
Gp.Fl.(4) 15 secs.

Ch. Spire

Tower

MAGNETIC NORTH

Var⁰ 7°6'W (1980)

Red

White

In Britain, the Admiralty regularly issues *Notices to Mariners* which features any alterations to be made to charts.

Depths

Look at a chart, and you will see that it is dotted with small figures. these indicate the 'least depth' of water in those areas.

If the area is tidal, the depth shown will be that at the lowest state of the tide (or 'low water', as sailors call it – high tide is 'high water'). This therefore, is the minimum depth usually to be found there. Depths are given in metres and centimetres.

A chart, therefore, will show you the least depth there is likely to be at any particular place. If you want to cross that area but it is too shallow for you to do so at low water, you will have to calculate when there will be enough water over it for you to make the passage. This is done by using tide-tables, which are rather like timetables of the sea, giving times of high and low tides and how much the water will rise between them. Comprehensive tide-tables are included in various nautical publications, but you should be able to get a simplified set for your particular area from your local club, boat shop or yacht yard.

You should, if possible, cross shoal areas on a rising tide. Then, if you do 'touch', you will soon float off again. You should also remember that, at sea, the shallower the water, the rougher it is likely to be.

Lead and line It is essential to have some means of checking how much water you have under you at any given time. This is called *taking soundings*, and previously it was always

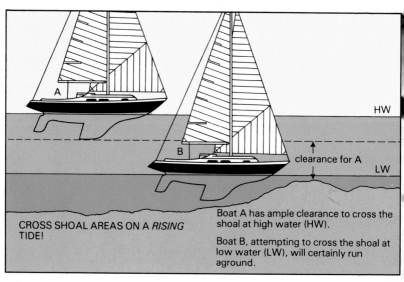

CROSS SHOAL AREAS ON A *RISING* TIDE!

Boat A has ample clearance to cross the shoal at high water (HW).

Boat B, attempting to cross the shoal at low water (LW), will certainly run aground.

done with a lead and line, which, as its description indicates, is simply a length of line with a lead weight at the end. The method of using it is to drop the lead over the side of the vessel and, when it touches bottom, read off the depth from markings on the line.

Scattered over the chart, like the figures representing depths, are small letters indicating the nature of the bottom – *s* for sand, *sh* for shingle, *m* for mud, and so on. A lead should have a cavity in the bottom filled with tallow or some other soft waterproof substance. Particles of sand and shingle will stick to this, indicating the nature of the bottom. This can be a very useful check on your position if you are not sure where you are.

Echo-sounders The lead and line method of taking soundings has now been largely superseded by an electronic device called an echo-sounder, which is far easier to use and which produces a continuous contour of the bottom of the water. It operates by transmitting an electrical impulse to the bottom which is returned as an echo, hence its name. From the time taken for the echo to return, the device calculates the depth to the bottom.

Echo-sounders are compact, comparatively cheap, and all you have to do to obtain soundings is to switch them on and read off the depths on a dial. It is a good idea, though, to have a lead and line in reserve, because it has one virtue the echo-sounder lacks. It cannot break down.

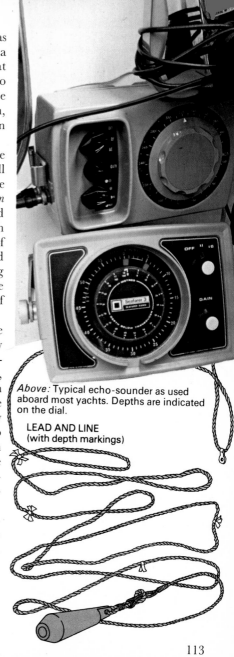

Above: Typical echo-sounder as used aboard most yachts. Depths are indicated on the dial.

LEAD AND LINE
(with depth markings)

Signposts of the sea

Charts also show navigational marks such as buoys, lightships and lighthouses, by which the sailors can steer or check the boat's position.

All important navigational marks have their own individual names, painted on them, and they all have special characteristics by which they can be identified both by day and by night. Such marks are represented on a chart by simplified, miniature drawings, accompanied by abbreviated descriptions of what they look like, and what they do.

Take as an example a buoy outside the important naval harbour at Portsmouth, on the south coast of England. This is represented on the

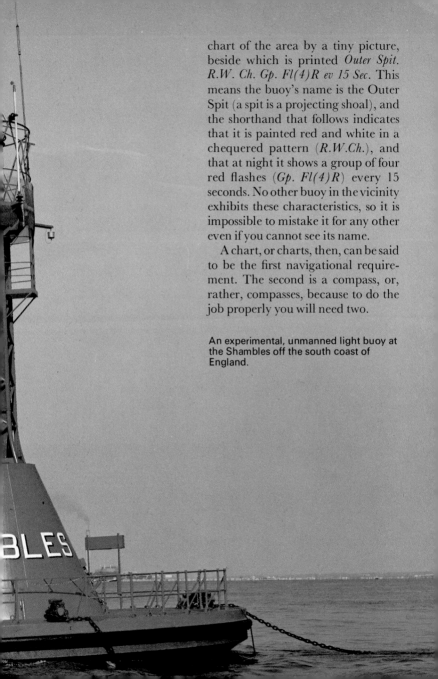

chart of the area by a tiny picture, beside which is printed *Outer Spit. R.W. Ch. Gp. Fl(4)R ev 15 Sec*. This means the buoy's name is the Outer Spit (a spit is a projecting shoal), and the shorthand that follows indicates that it is painted red and white in a chequered pattern (*R.W.Ch.*), and that at night it shows a group of four red flashes (*Gp. Fl(4)R*) every 15 seconds. No other buoy in the vicinity exhibits these characteristics, so it is impossible to mistake it for any other even if you cannot see its name.

A chart, or charts, then, can be said to be the first navigational requirement. The second is a compass, or, rather, compasses, because to do the job properly you will need two.

An experimental, unmanned light buoy at the Shambles off the south coast of England.

Compasses

A compass is an instrument which indicates direction. It has two uses, which is why you require two. Firstly, you need one to tell you which way the boat should head when you cannot see any marks to steer by. The other is to show in which direction, relative to the boat, navigational marks lie when you can see them.

You may think that you do not need a compass at all if you are just going to sail in a river estuary, or along the coast. But a sea mist may come in, or even a heavy rainstorm, and your visual marks will be obliterated. It would be only too easy then, without a compass, to stray off-course until you end up on a sandbank.

There are several kinds of compass. Nowadays ships use electrical ones which indicate directions with reference to the North Pole, which is known as *true north*. They used to use magnetic compasses, and most small boats still do. These indicate directions with reference to *magnetic north*, which is near true north.

A magnetic compass consists basically of a magnetic needle which always points north. The idea is that if you know where north is, you can tell where east, south and west are. These, and other intermediate directions, are in fact indicated on a circular card attached to the magnetic needle. This card, called the compass card, floats in a bowl of liquid, so that the needle is free to point north whichever way the boat may turn.

The bridge of a modern container ship. It has a range of instruments which are much more complex than the simple magnetic compass used on a sailing boat.

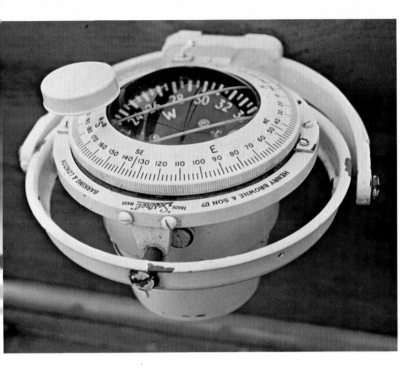

The bowl itself is suspended in gymbals so that it will remain level, whatever the motion of the boat.

Steering compass

The compass card will probably have two sets of markings around its circumference. On the outside it will be divided into the 360° of a circle, running clockwise from 0° at North. A ring just inside this will show directions in the traditional 'points' notation of north, north-east, southwest, and so on. This is easy enough to steer by until you come down to such subdivisions as south-west-by-south or east-by-north. On the whole it is

Steering compass. The bowl of the compass is suspended on a frame so that it can swing freely and remain level whichever way the boat moves.

easier to steer by the degree system.

A steering compass has one other essential. You need to know not only in which direction north, south, east and west are, but also in which direction the boat is heading. You can get some idea simply by looking at the compass card, but you need to be more accurate than that.

This accuracy is obtained by the fore-and-aft line of the boat – the line along which she is heading – being indicated by a mark on the inside of

the compass bowl. This is known as the *lubber line*. If you keep the direction on the compass in which you wish to steer exactly on the lubber line, then the boat will be heading precisely in that direction. For example, if you wish to head due south, you line up south (or 180°) on the compass card with the lubber line.

The steering compass will be positioned in the cockpit in such a way that the helmsman will be able to see it easily from his or her steering position. At night the compass card will be illuminated from the bottom of the bowl.

Bearing compass
It may be possible to take rough bearings (check the general direction) of

The steering compass on this large yacht is so positioned that the helmsman always has a clear view of it without having to move.

visual marks using the steering compass, but it is most unlikely that it will be so situated that you can make accurate observations with it.

This means using a bearing compass, or, to give it its full name, a hand bearing compass, so-called for the simple reason that it is held in the hand.

A bearing compass is similar to a steering compass but smaller. It has a spigot-type handle underneath which also serves as a housing for an electric battery to light up the compass at night.

There is a line on the inside of the bowl like the lubber line on a steering

Hold the compass at eye-level, pointing at the object, with the prism on the far side. Sight along the lubber line and read off the bearing.

HAND BEARING COMPASS

compass, and in addition a glass prism, on the rim of the bowl above the lubber line, which magnifies the part of the card immediately beneath it, making it easier to read the markings on it.

To take a bearing of an object, for example a navigation buoy, the compass is held at eye-level with the prism on the far side, pointing in the direction of the buoy of which the bearing is being taken. There is a notch in the prism. Sighting along the lubber line, the notch in the prism is lined up with the buoy, then the marking on the compass card immediately below the prism is read off. This is the bearing of the buoy from where you are.

Fixing a position

A bearing can just be a rough check of your position. You may look at the chart and say, 'If the bearing of that is this, then we must be about *here*'. This may be useful, especially if you are on a definite course and merely want to confirm how much progress you have made along it.

But often 'about here' is not good enough. You will need to check your position more precisely and to do this you will have to take more than one bearing.

This is called 'fixing a position', or 'taking a fix', and requires actual work on the chart. This is why you need a flat surface – that board covering the washing-up area, unless you are lucky enough to have a proper chart table. All navigational work on a chart should be done in pencil, so that it can be erased and the chart re-used.

Fixing a position involves using a parallel ruler and also the compass roses on the chart. A parallel ruler is a device which can be moved across a flat surface such as an outspread chart without altering its lie or angle. There are two main types: the bar ruler, which is really two rulers joined together, which can be 'walked' across the chart; and a rod-like kind, which is rolled along. The bar ruler is the more popular of the two, because it is possible to draw lines with it more accurately. Its twin rulers are joined by pivoted crosspieces in such a way

that, by moving first one ruler and then the other, you can keep the whole thing pointing in the direction it started from.

The first step in fixing a position is to take a bearing of some object marked on the chart. It should be some distance away. (The greater the distance, the more accurate the bearing is likely to be.) Next represent this bearing by a line on the chart. This is done by laying the parallel ruler across the nearest compass rose so that it passes exactly through the centre of the rose and cuts the circumference, on the bearing you have taken. You then walk the ruler across the chart until its edge cuts through the object of which you have taken the bearing.

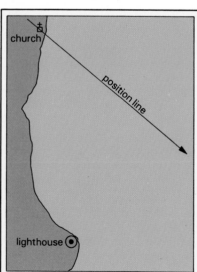

Taking one bearing establishes your approximate position.

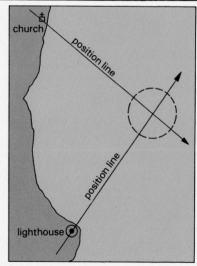

Taking two bearings establishes your position more precisely.

Then draw a line, with the ruler, from the object towards and well beyond your likely position.

This is known as a *position line*, and if you are sailing on a given course, perhaps one marked on the chart, it may be all you need. Where the bearing line cuts your course-line will be your position at that time.

If you are not sailing on a known course, all that one position line will tell you is that you are somewhere along it. You may know roughly where, but in order to fix your position precisely, you will have to take a bearing of another object. You then go through the same procedure of transferring the bearing to the chart in the form of a second position line, and where this second line crosses the first will be – if you have done it right – your position!

The second object of which you take a bearing should be as nearly as possible at 90° degrees to the first, because if the position lines cross at right-angles, the position obtained will be more accurate than if the two lines have only a small angle between them.

Cocked hat

If, having taken two bearings and transferred them to the chart, you are still in doubt where you are, you may decide to take a third. Because of the difficulty of taking absolutely accurate bearings from a small boat, which may be moving about a great deal, it is unlikely that the third position line will pass exactly through

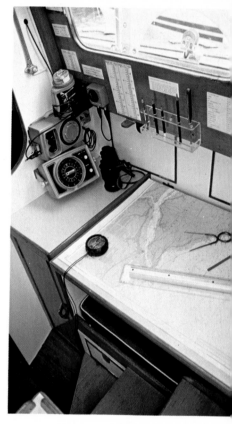

A workmanlike chart table, with everything to hand. The main requirement is a flat surface to work on.

the point of intersection of the first two. Instead, a small triangle, known navigationally as a cocked hat, will be formed, and you will know that you are somewhere within this area.

The smaller the cocked hat, the more accurate your fix. If it is too large, you will have to take one or more of your bearings again.

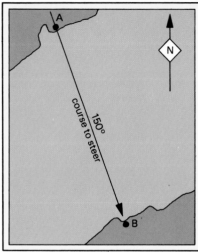
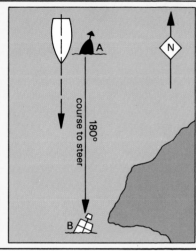

Laying off a course

Working out the direction in which to steer from one point to another is called laying off a course. This also requires the use of a parallel ruler and reference to a compass rose.

Suppose you are at a position we will call point A, and you want to find the course to steer to point B. Start by drawing, with the parallel ruler, a straight line on the chart between these two points, checking at the same time that there are no obstacles along the way. Then walk the ruler across the chart to the nearest compass rose until the edge of the ruler passes exactly through the rose's centre. The point at which the edge of the ruler cuts the circumference of the rose gives the bearing of the course you want to steer.

Laying off a course is therefore rather like taking a bearing in reverse. Instead of working from the compass rose and then drawing a line on the chart, draw the line first, then refer it to the rose.

You can do a very simple exercise in laying off a course. All you have to do is choose two navigational marks in your vicinity which are shown on your chart. Suppose that they are two buoys, buoy A, and buoy B. Draw a line with your parallel ruler from buoy A to buoy B. Now walk the ruler across to the nearest compass rose until its edge cuts the rose's centre, and lay off the course to sail from buoy A to buoy B. Let us assume it turns out to be south, or 180°. Sail up to buoy A and alter course until the lubber line on the bowl of the steering compass is exactly against 180°. Buoy B should be dead ahead.

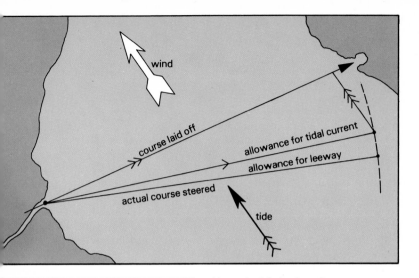

wind

course laid off

allowance for tidal current

allowance for leeway

actual course steered

tide

Allowing for weather

Above, far left: Laying off a course between two points.

Above, left: Laying off a course between two buoys.

Above: Allowing for weather when laying off a course. After allowing for tidal current and leeway, the course steered may appear to be taking you away from your destination!

You should now know how to steer, how to fix a position, and how to lay off a course, but this is only the basis of the business. You must also take into consideration the direction of the wind relative to the course, and the fact that, if you are sailing on the sea, or even a river, the water you are sailing through will itself be moving. Both may considerably modify the actual course you have to steer to reach a given objective, and how far you get in a given time.

It has already been mentioned that the oblique pressure of the wind causes leeway, and that this will vary according to the point of sailing. This sideways component can be calculated and, by means of a geometric diagram, a new course line can be drawn to give the direction to steer to allow for leeway. In local, 'point-to-point' sailing, however, this is really an unnecessary refinement because the required allowance for leeway can be estimated instead of calculated. In such circumstances conditions are liable to change so frequently anyway that calculation is scarcely practicable.

The movement of the water you are sailing through is mainly due to tides and tidal streams (which may be described as currents in the sea).

Tides

Tides are movements of the sea caused by the gravitational pull of the Moon, and, to a lesser degree, the Sun. The Sun has less effect because, in spite of it being so much larger than the Moon, it is very much further away.

In most places on the Earth's surface, high tide (high water), and low tide (low water), occur twice every lunar day, the duration of which is roughly 24 hours and 50 minutes.

Three things about tides concern us: their times; their range: and their direction and rate of flow.

Times of tides can be ascertained by reference to tide-tables. These give the times of high water at a particular place and the time differences from that for other places. Tide-tables for Britain, for example, give the times of high water at Dover, and how much earlier or later high water is at other places around the coast. Using tide-tables, the times of the tides almost anywhere in the world can be discovered.

Tidal range

The *vertical* difference (difference in depth) between high and low water is called the tide's range. This must not be confused with how far it comes in

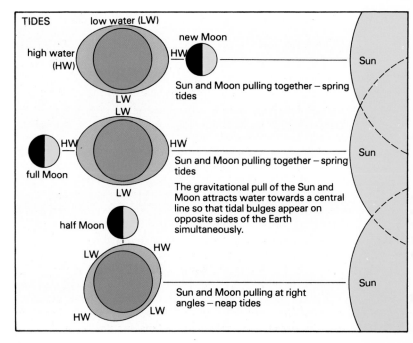

TIDES

high water (HW) / low water (LW)

new Moon
HW
Sun and Moon pulling together – spring tides

full Moon
HW
Sun and Moon pulling together – spring tides

The gravitational pull of the Sun and Moon attracts water towards a central line so that tidal bulges appear on opposite sides of the Earth simultaneously.

half Moon
HW
Sun and Moon pulling at right angles – neap tides

Sun

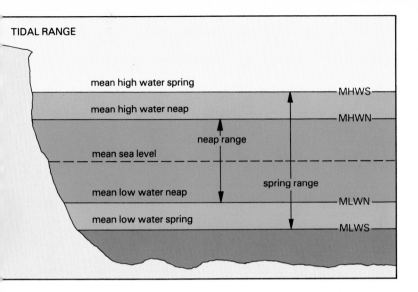

TIDAL RANGE

mean high water spring — MHWS

mean high water neap — MHWN

neap range

mean sea level

spring range

mean low water neap — MLWN

mean low water spring — MLWS

or goes out, which will obviously be more on a flat shore than a steep one, although the range may be the same.

The range of the tide varies not only from place to place, but also according to the day of the lunar month. When the Moon and the Sun are pulling in the same direction, which happens around new moon and full moon, the result is a tide of maximum range.

These tides are called *spring tides*, perhaps because they 'spring' higher than the ones in between. They also fall further at low tide. Spring tides have nothing to do with the season of the year, but occur twice every lunar month.

After causing spring tides, the Moon and the Sun move gradually more and more out of line, until they are pulling at right angles to each other. The range of the tides decreases, reaching a minimum at the time of the *neap tides*, which also occur twice every lunar month, alternating with the spring tides. There is a regular, repetitive rhythm about the tides, which increase gradually from neaps to springs, then decrease gradually to neaps again.

Because spring tides have further to rise than neaps, they run more strongly (the higher the tide, the faster the rate of flow), which may be a help or a hindrance, depending on which way you are going. Neap tides run less strongly and also do not fall as far as spring tides, which again may be an advantage or the reverse. For example, if you are moving with the tide, you will not get as much help from neaps as springs, but if you are going against it, you will not be held

TIDAL STREAMS AROUND THE ISLE OF WIGHT, ENGLAND (speed in knots)

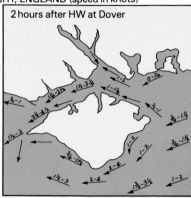

at time of high water at Dover

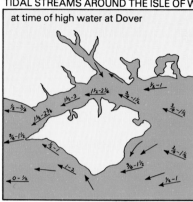

2 hours after HW at Dover

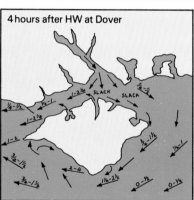

4 hours after HW at Dover

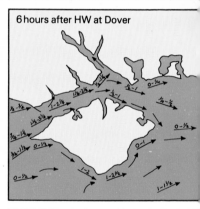

6 hours after HW at Dover

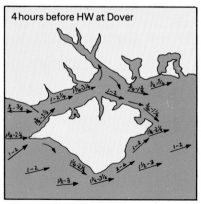

4 hours before HW at Dover

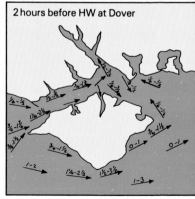

2 hours before HW at Dover

ack as much. Or there may be enough water over a shallow patch at neap low tides which will enable you to take a short cut which would not be possible at spring low tides (a rather tricky procedure, this, and you should really know the area well and study your chart carefully before attempting it).

Tidal streams

These currents in the sea are often losely associated with tides and share many of their characteristics. They too are caused by the pull of the Moon and the Sun, vary according to the position of those heavenly bodies, and are equally predictable. Most of them also move for a certain period in one direction, then turn, just like the tide, and go the opposite way.

Tidal streams can do a great deal to help you on your way. A good example is the really big one which floods in from the Atlantic Ocean round the British Isles, which divide it in two. One part of the stream runs up the English Channel and the other comes in round the north of Scotland and down the east coast of England. The two branches meet in the English Channel, not far from Dover, then turn round and go back the way they came. The notorious, ever-shifting Goodwin Sands are caused by the meeting of these streams.

Obviously, if you want to make a passage round the coast of Britain, it will help a lot if you can take advantage of this 'lift' on your way. If, for example, you are sailing eastwards

up the English Channel at 5 knots (a knot being a speed of one nautical mile per hour), and the tidal stream is moving the same way at 2 knots, then your actual 'speed over the ground' as sailors call it, (the speed at which you are approaching your objective) will be 7 knots. If the tidal stream is moving at 2 knots in the opposite direction, your speed over the ground will be 5 knots minus 2 knots, so it will only be 3 knots over the ground.

Tidal movements are of equal importance in creeks and rivers. When the tide rises (floods), it flows up into these inlets, and when it falls (ebbs), it runs out again. A rising tide, is called a *flood tide*, and a falling tide an *ebb tide*. Where a river empties into the sea, the additional speed of the river flow usually makes the ebb tide much faster than the flood tide.

A good sailor who wants to make a fast passage will always try to 'work the tides'; that is, take as much advantage of them as you can. If you want to head out to sea from a creek or river, you should aim to do so on the ebb tide. If you want to go further inland, leave on the flood tide. Set out not by the clock, but when the tide serves you best, even if it means getting out of your bunk at some horribly early hour.

Also, work out in advance whether you want to take advantage of the whole or part of a tide. If you want to get as far as possible in the direction the tide is running, you can use the whole of it. But if all you are going to do is sail out of one creek and up another some distance up the coast, you will still want to leave on the ebb, but you won't want to get to the entrance to the other creek before the tide has turned and started to flood up into it. You could then leave when the ebb tide has run, say, half its course, that is, at *half-ebb*. You should then arrive at the entrance to your destination creek just as the tide turns in your favour and floods into the creek.

Another factor which may affect the situation is that tides and tidal streams run at varying rates during their 6 hours of rising or falling. At high and low tide, when they are on the turn, there is little or no movement, and this is known as *slack water* – which may be a good time to arrive off a harbour with a tricky entrance. The tide will then run, slowly at first, but increasing to maximum speed at about half-ebb or half-flood, after which the rate will decrease to the next slack water.

What use you make of tides and tidal streams will also depend on other circumstances such as the direction and strength of the wind. If the tide will be against you when you get under away, but on the other hand you have a fresh and favourable wind, you will probably want to set off anyway. Sailing is usually a matter of weighing up the advantages and disadvantages.

Tidal streams are often shown on charts as insets with arrows indicating the direction in which they run. Their average rate in knots is printed along the shaft of the arrow.

Yachts drifting along on a very calm day. The flow round the buoy is a sign that they are moving upstream with the tide.

Buoyage system

The navigational marks that matter most to small-boat sailors are buoys. Identification of these from charts has already been described but not much has been said about their purpose.

There are two main kinds of buoy – those which mark the sides of navigable channels, and those which mark dangers such as wrecks and rocks.

Channel buoys

Channel buoys differ in shape and colour according to whether they are on the port or starboard side of the channel *when a vessel is coming in from seaward.*

Buoyage systems differ, at present, throughout the world. An international system has been introduced and is expected to be in use throughout British waters by December 1981. Under this system, buoys marking the right or starboard-hand side of a channel are pointed (the official description is conical), and painted green, while buoys marking the left or port-hand side are drum-shaped (can-shaped), and are painted red.

At intervals the buoys marking a channel may have erections on top, known as *top-marks,* such as a cone, a diamond, or a cross. Some will also exhibit lights. The buoys will be shown on the chart, and they may also be numbered from seaward, with the odd numbers on the starboard side, even numbers on the port side. These numbers can be a considerable help if the buoy has no other characteristics apart from its shape and colour. For instance, if you are trying to find your way in from sea on a dark and dirty night and come

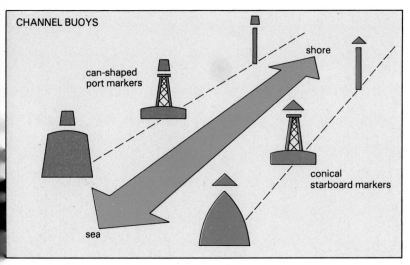

CHANNEL BUOYS

can-shaped port markers

shore

conical starboard markers

sea

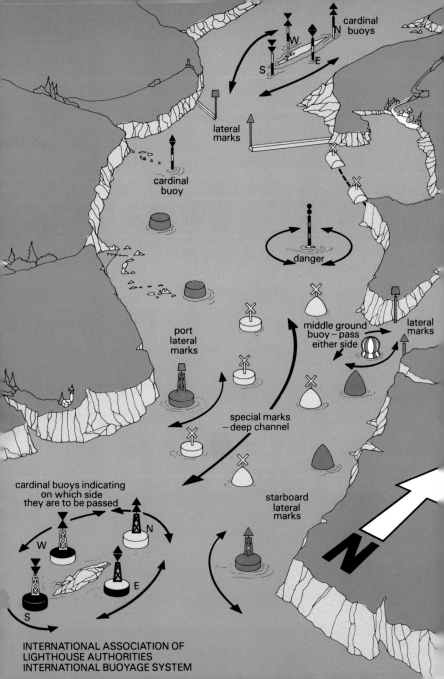

cardinal
buoys

N

W

S

E

lateral
marks

cardinal
buoy

danger

lateral
marks

port
lateral
marks

middle ground
buoy – pass
either side

special marks
– deep channel

cardinal buoys indicating
on which side
they are to be passed

W

N

E

S

starboard
lateral
marks

N

INTERNATIONAL ASSOCIATION OF
LIGHTHOUSE AUTHORITIES
INTERNATIONAL BUOYAGE SYSTEM

across a starboard-hand buoy with the number '13' painted on it, you will be able to pin-point where you are by looking at your chart.

Other channel markings Minor channels in creeks, rivers and so on are usually marked with sticks or branches of trees, called withies, stuck into the shallow water on either side. Needless to say, none of these marks are lit, so navigating such channels in any but the most familiar of surroundings and on the clearest of nights is not to be recommended.

Below: A creek with withies marking the shallow water on each side.

Other buoys

When navigating a channel, you may also come across what are called 'middle-ground' buoys. These mark shallow water in the middle of a channel. They are usually round, and can be passed on either side. Their characteristics will be shown on the chart.

Under the international system, danger buoys will be black and red. Lights, if present, will be white.

Lights Buoys (and some other navigational marks) which show lights are divided into various categories according to the way the light shines. They may be either *fixed*, in which case they will shine steadily all the time; or *flashing*, when they will flash a given number of times during a certain period of time (if the flashes come in groups, it will be a *group-flashing* light). There are also *occulting* lights, which, instead of flashing, go dark. In other words they shine for the greater part of the time and go out in accordance with a sequence fixed for that particular buoy. As with flashing lights, the moments or periods of darkness may be single or occur in groups. In the first case they will be occulting and in the second *group-occulting*.

Sound signals Some buoys could be called 'fog buoys', since in addition to their identification by shape, colour and lights, they also make sound signals. This may be either a diaphone, which is a foghorn-type device, or a whistle or bell activated by the movement of the sea.

Lighthouses and lightships

All major navigational marks such as lighthouses and lightships are also equipped with sound signals, for example a powerful diaphone emitting a loud, moaning sound which ends in a grunt.

Information about the characteristics of lighthouses and lightships is printed near them on the chart just as it is with buoys. There is additional information about the height of the light above sea level and how far it is visible in clear weather, both of which enable the navigator to estimate how far away the light is.

You may also see, if you look at the representation of a lighthouse on a chart, that part of the arc or circle indicating the light is coloured red. This simply means 'danger'. If, from your point of observation, a lighthouse beam is flashing red, then you are 'standing into danger', or, in other words, heading for a hazard of some kind.

So far only the marks and lights by which vessels can navigate have been discussed. There are also markings by which vessels identify themselves and, if necessary, indicate what they are doing. This subject is covered by the *International Collision Regulations*.

The Fastnet lighthouse, situated off the south-west coast of Ireland, warns of the dangers of rocks.

132

International Collision Regulations

These could be described as a 'Seaway Code' – a sort of Highway Code for sailors. Obviously there have to be rules for the movement of vessels on the water just as there are for vehicles on land.

In all there are 31 rules, some of them simple, some quite complicated. These rules are international. In Britain, they are published in booklet form by HMSO (Her Majesty's Stationery Office), and are also included in a number of other nautical publications. They are therefore readily obtainable.

The International Collision Regulations, like the land travellers' Highway Code, are aimed primarily at avoiding collisions. They lay down which vessel has the right-of-way in various situations. Some important examples are given.

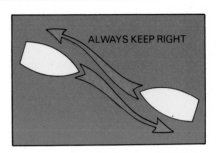

ALWAYS KEEP RIGHT

Conduct of vessels under way in sight of one another

Keep right

When two vessels are approaching each other head-on both should, if possible, alter course to starboard: in other words, **keep to the right.**

If for any reason one or both vessels is unable to alter course to starboard – perhaps they are approaching each other in a very narrow channel – then appropriate action must be taken to avoid a collision. One vessel may even have to go astern (backwards).

A word of warning to small-boat sailors. You would be unwise to rely on large vessels observing this rule where you are concerned. They may think you should not be where you are and expect you to get out of the way – or they may not even have seen you. Their size may also prevent them from moving out of the channel they are navigating. The golden rule in such a situation is: keep out of the way!

Power driven vessels

A vessel under way under power (being propelled by an engine or engines) is required to keep out of the way of one under sail.

This is obviously only common sense since a vessel with an engine is usually more manoeuvrable than one which is dependent on the wind. Again, though, you would be unwise to try and assert your right-of-way if the other vessel is much bigger than you. Once more, the most sensible thing to do is to keep out of the way.

Overtaking

A vessel overtaking another must keep clear of the vessel being overtaken. This is logical, since the faster a vessel is moving, the more power and general manoeuvrability she is likely to have.

Sailing vessels

The rule governing the conduct of sailing vessels is probably the most important of all the Regulations as far as you are concerned, because it deals with sailing vessels in collision situations, and sailing vessels are the ones you are most likely to encounter or be in company with.

The rule states that, when two sailing vessels are approaching each other in such a way that there is a risk of collision, one of them shall keep out of the way of the other.

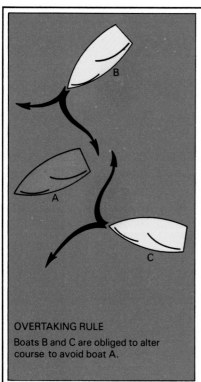

OVERTAKING RULE

Boats B and C are obliged to alter course to avoid boat A.

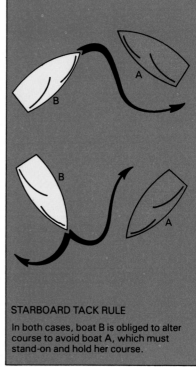

STARBOARD TACK RULE

In both cases, boat B is obliged to alter course to avoid boat A, which must stand-on and hold her course.

Wind on different sides When the two vessels have the wind on different sides, the vessel which has the wind on the port side shall keep out of the way of the other. (That is to say, the vessel on the starboard tack has the right of way, as mentioned in the discussion of racing tactics.)

Wind on the same side When both vessels have the wind on the same side (in other words, when they are both on the same tack), the vessel which is to windward (nearer the wind) shall keep clear of the vessel which is to the leeward. This is logical because, generally speaking, the windward vessel will be the more manoeuvrable of the two. She will have a free wind whereas the one to leeward may have her wind taken by the windward vessel's sails. Also, if the wind is blowing onshore (towards the land), the vessel to leeward will be nearer to the land and will therefore have less room to manoeuvre.

If a vessel with the wind on the port side sees a vessel to windward, but cannot tell whether it has the wind on the port or starboard side, she should keep out of the way.

Avoiding action

When one vessel takes avoiding action, it should be done in such an obvious way that the other can be in no doubt as to what is happening. A slight alteration in course is not enough, even if that would take you safely past. It should be marked, even exaggerated, so that it is clearly visible to the other vessel. And it should be done in plenty of time, when the two vessels are still a good distance apart.

In this sort of situation, the vessel which has the right of way also has to behave in a manner specifically laid down. It is her duty to 'stand on', which means she must not change course, nor, except in certain circumstances, alter her speed. This is because the vessel which has to take avoiding action may not be able to do

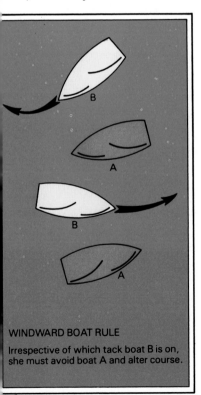

WINDWARD BOAT RULE
Irrespective of which tack boat B is on, she must avoid boat A and alter course.

so safely if she does not know what the other one is going to do.

Identification of vessels

Many of the provisions of the Regulations are concerned with the identification of vessels both by day and night, and with visual indications of what they are doing.

Vessels engaged in specific activities, such as cable-laying or fishing, are required by the Regulations to exhibit lights or shapes indicating those activities. You do not have to know all these by heart, but it would be useful to have the means of looking them up.

Lights

At night, power vessels are required to display a white light or lights at or near the masthead. These indicate how big they are. If they are under 45 metres long they show one white light, and if they are longer than that, they have two.

All vessels under way are required to carry navigation lights as follows: they must have a green light visible to

NAVIGATION LIGHTS

A. Tricolour masthead light for sailing craft with a length under 12m.
B. Sailing with a combined port and starboard pulpit light plus stern light for a craft also under 12m.
C. Boats under power (as these 3 boats), including those with sails hoisted, should show a white masthead light.
D. Large sailing yachts may have red over green lights at the masthead, but in combination with side and stern lights.

A

D

C

C

137

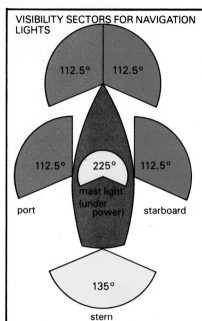

Above: Combined port and starboard pulpit light.

starboard from ahead on that side; a red light similarly visible to port; a white light visible from astern. The point of these lights is that you can tell which way the vessel is moving by which of them you can see, and they must therefore be shielded so that they shine only in their prescribed direction.

Very small craft such as dinghies are not obliged to carry these lights, but for your own safety, you should have some visual means of indicating your presence when necessary. The best thing for this purpose is an electric torch (make sure it works and shows a good light), and the best way to use it is to shine it not at the other vessel but on your mainsail, lighting up as much of it as possible.

You may think that you can see what the other vessel is doing, but even in daylight and good visibility it is not quite so easy as that. The ship you think is coming towards you may be lying at anchor, or vice versa. Certain of the Regulations prevent misunderstandings of this kind. In the situation described, a vessel at anchor is required to exhibit, during the hours of daylight, a black ball, or a *shape*, as it is called, somewhere in the forepart of the vessel, near the bows. It will be hoisted in the rigging, so that it can be clearly seen. At night the black ball, which would not be

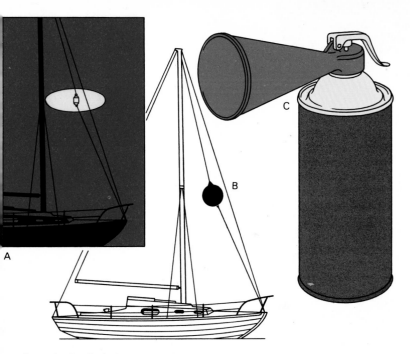

much use in the dark, is replaced by a white light in the same place.

Sound signals

Vessels indicate their presence, and what they are doing, not only visually but also by sound signals. A short blast on a ship's siren indicates that she is about to turn to starboard, two blasts that she is turning to port, and three blasts that she is going astern. In fog she will sound one long blast every two minutes when under way, two long blasts when standing still (not moving through the water, but not moored or at anchor), and a sequence of short-long-short blasts every minute when she is at anchor. Small

A. Vessel anchored at night, showing rigging light.

B. Vessel anchored during the day, showing black ball.

C. Aerosol-type foghorn, operated by pressing the lever.

sailing vessels make similar signals, usually with a foghorn, or, failing that, anything that happens to be at hand – drumming on the bottom of a saucepan will be better than nothing. The important thing is to tell people the boat is there. An aerosol-type foghorn is very useful.

Safety Afloat

It has already been pointed out that sailing can be a dangerous sport; that you can drown, or suffer injury if you are foolhardy, or do not know what you are doing. But you can do a great deal to reduce the element of danger. As long as you really know what you are about, and take the proper precautions, you should not find sailing any more hazardous than most other outdoor activities.

This question of safety depends to some extent on what kind of boat you are sailing, and where you are sailing.

Lifejackets are essential items of safety equipment and must be worn at all times in sailing dinghies.

PUTTING ON A LIFEJACKET

1. Put the lifejacket on over your head.

2. Fasten the tapes round from the back to the front.

3. Inflate the lifejacket.

4. If you end up in the water, the lifejacket will keep you floating head up.

Lifejackets

The old-fashioned lifebelt has more or less disappeared, and so has the cork variety which you had to put on over your head and then tie round your waist with tapes.

Modern lifejackets are more like garments and are useful as an added protection in cold and wet weather, but of course their main purpose is to save life, and their efficiency in this respect is all-important.

A lifejacket must be buoyant enough to support the wearer's whole weight, in case, because of injury or for some other reason, he is unable to keep himself afloat. It must also be designed to support the wearer, even if he is unconscious, with his nose and mouth well clear of the water. Finally, it should be of a colour that shows up well, preferably orange or yellow.

It should go without saying that the jacket must be in good condition. One that comes unfastened and rides up over the wearer's head when he is in the water will obviously be more of a hazard than a help.

There must always, in both dinghies and larger craft, be someone in command. Someone has got to make decisions, and those decisions must be accepted and obeyed. If the skipper says that you must all wear your lifejackets, then you all wear your lifejackets. If people do not bring their own lifejackets with them, there must be a sufficient number on board for everyone.

Safety in dinghies

Capsizes

The main difference between dinghies and larger boats is that dinghies will capsize and larger boats will not, except in extreme conditions.

A capsize will almost certainly mean ending up in the water, and for this reason **all dinghy sailors must at all times wear lifejackets.** It doesn't matter how calm and safe the weather may seem.

The degree of danger involved in a capsize may also depend on the weather and where you are sailing. Quite plainly your situation is going to be

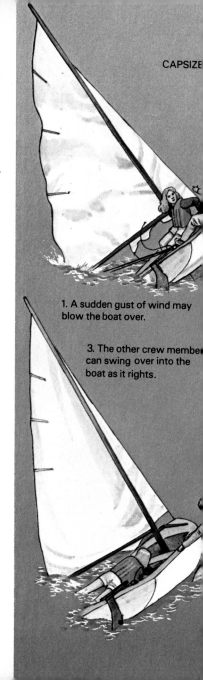

CAPSIZE

1. A sudden gust of wind may blow the boat over.

3. The other crew member can swing over into the boat as it rights.

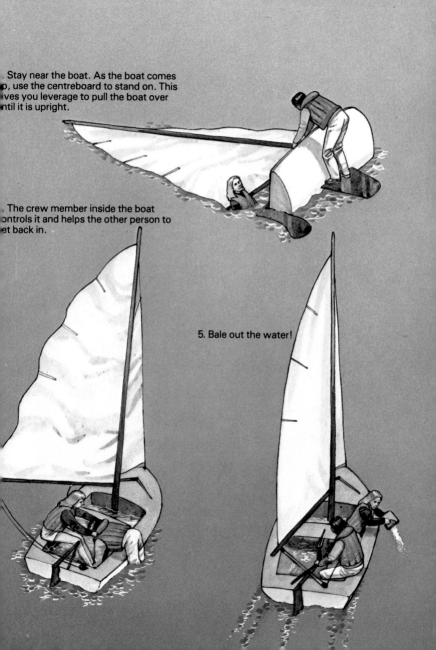

Stay near the boat. As the boat comes up, use the centreboard to stand on. This gives you leverage to pull the boat over until it is upright.

The crew member inside the boat controls it and helps the other person to get back in.

5. Bale out the water!

trickier in a strong wind with a rough sea and a fast tide running than it would be on an inland waterway on a calm day. But, whatever the situation, the same basic rule should be applied – **stay with the boat.** Hang on to it. Virtually all dinghies will float even when capsized or full of water, and will add to the support you are getting from your lifejacket. And, hanging on to the boat, you will be a lot easier for a rescue boat to locate.

The main danger if you are pitched into the water when sailing a dinghy is that you will come up under a sail lying on the surface. The important thing in such a situation is d

A capsized dinghy which is just being righted. Fortunately the boat isn't water-logged and the crew should soon be back on board and sailing again.

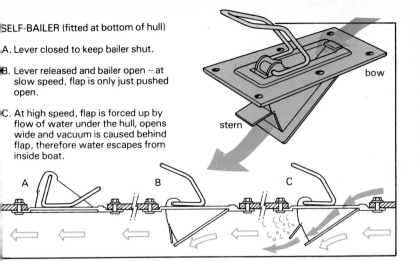

SELF-BAILER (fitted at bottom of hull)

A. Lever closed to keep bailer shut.

B. Lever released and bailer open – at slow speed, flap is only just pushed open.

C. At high speed, flap is forced up by flow of water under the hull, opens wide and vacuum is caused behind flap, therefore water escapes from inside boat.

bow

stern

A   B   C

not panic. As long as you realize what has happened and keep your wits about you, you will be able to extricate yourself all right.

In waters where there may be sharks, some people recommend getting on top of the mainsail as some degree of protection while you are waiting to be picked up.

It is common for dinghy crews to right their craft themselves after a capsize. This can be done by standing on the keel, holding on to the side of the boat or the rigging, and leaning back to exert as much leverage as possible, more or less as one does when 'sitting out' a boat to balance her. The problem is that, since a boat full of water is extremely unstable, you may get her upright only to have her capsize again, the other way, on top of you. You may have to take the sails or at least the mainsail down before you attempt this manoeuvre

Capsizing is *not* fun. A recent survey showed that over a quarter of all small boat drownings in the United States result from capsizes.

Maintenance

It is also essential that your boat is 'well-found', which is a nautical expression meaning sound and in good working order. A fraying shroud which has not been replaced could result in the boat being dismasted. A loose rudder could come adrift so that you will not be able to steer, or a centreboard could stick so you will not be able to go to windward and could end up on a lee shore.

If any of these things happened at sea, you might well find yourself in trouble, and even on a river or a lake the results could be serious. In any case, you may progress to more ambitious sailing later on. You should learn the habit of safety.

Boarding a large boat

Mention should also be made of safety in the little boats, propelled by oars or small outboard motors, which are used to get to and from larger craft. Every sailing season a number of accidents happen in these which should never happen at all.

The main cause is overloading the boats with people and gear. It could take only the wake of a passing vessel to swamp an overloaded boat. The second dangerous situation is coming alongside the larger boat. If there is a free-for-all to get on board, with everybody standing up, the dinghy could slide away from under them. The correct drill is for only one person to transfer at a time while the others hold on to the larger boat.

The dinghy should be secured to some part of the 'parent' boat by her *painter* (the rope attached to the dinghy's bows) before anyone boards at all. Otherwise you may forget all about her, and she may drift away.

BOARDING A LARGE BOAT
Secure the dinghy to the boat. Only one person at a time should board, while the others hold on to the larger boat.

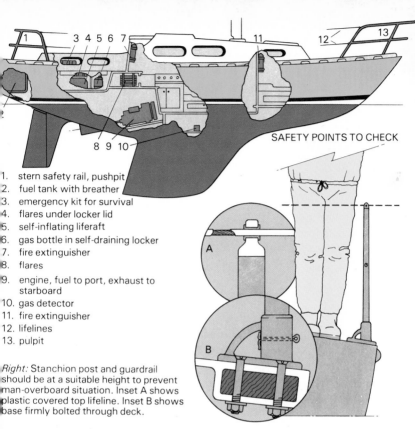

1. stern safety rail, pushpit
2. fuel tank with breather
3. emergency kit for survival
4. flares under locker lid
5. self-inflating liferaft
6. gas bottle in self-draining locker
7. fire extinguisher
8. flares
9. engine, fuel to port, exhaust to starboard
10. gas detector
11. fire extinguisher
12. lifelines
13. pulpit

Right: Stanchion post and guardrail should be at a suitable height to prevent man-overboard situation. Inset A shows plastic covered top lifeline. Inset B shows base firmly bolted through deck.

SAFETY POINTS TO CHECK

Safety in cabin boats

It is even more important for a cabin boat to be well-found because she is likely to have to take more of a battering from the wind and waves. The failure of any part of her structure or equipment may have more serious consequences than it would in the case of a dinghy because she may be further from land and therefore from any source of help when it happens.

Everything must be strong enough to do the job it is meant to do, and all the working parts must work properly. Objects should be kept in convenient places, ready to be used. For example, fire extinguishers should be within easy reach of anything likely to go up in flames – the cooking stove or engine. All movables must be stowed or lashed so that they will stay put when the boat is heeling to the wind or pitching. This applies not only down below but on deck as well. Anchor chains should be made fast and anchors carefully stowed.

Fire and explosion

If a boat has an engine or a cooking stove, then there is a very definite fire-risk, and precautions against it must be taken.

Fire-extinguishers must be kept handy, somewhere near, but not too near, the most likely sources of trouble. If, for example, the cooking stove catches fire, you will then be able to reach the extinguisher without first having to try to get at it through the fire.

Check from time to time that extinguishers are charged and work properly. They would not be much use if they are empty or the stuff inside will not come out.

Check also from time to time that neither your fuel reservoirs, nor any supply lines leading from them, have developed leaks, and that everything is still properly secured.

Take great care not to over-fill engine fuel tanks, paraffin stove reservoirs, or even riding lights, if you use the paraffin kind. Any spillage will probably get down into the bilges

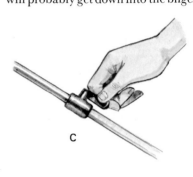

C

B

A

FIRE PREVENTION

A. Always use a funnel to avoid fuel spills.

B. Turn off gas at the cylinder after use.

C. Turn off the fuel supply from the tank.

the bottom of the boat, under the floor-boards) where it may vaporize and create the danger of an explosion (the same applies to leakages from gas cylinders). Gadgets can be obtained which give warning of the presence of dangerous fumes, but while it may be a good idea to have one of these, it is much more important to observe the precautions which will make such a thing unnecessary.

When you have finished using your engine, always turn off the fuel at the main tap on the tank. It is a good idea to switch off by turning off the fuel at

the tank and just letting the engine run out to use up any fuel between the tank and the engine (only if it is a petrol engine – **never do this with a diesel engine**).

If you have a gas stove with a fuel line, always switch off the gas at the cylinder after use.

Below: Putting out a fire. Fire extinguishers should be easily and safely accessible. Direct nozzles of extinguishers at base of flame. If the fire is caused by fat burning in a pan, never throw water on it but cover the pan until you can get the fire extinguisher.

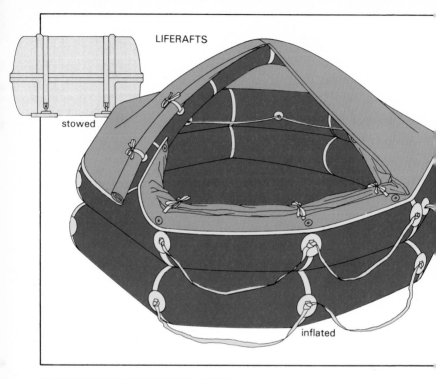

LIFERAFTS

stowed

inflated

Lifeboats

Every vessel should carry a lifeboat of
some kind. It may be a dinghy or it
may be a specially designed liferaft.

An ordinary rigid wooden or GRP
dinghy is unlikely to survive in very
bad conditions, especially if there are
several people crowded into it. An
inflatable rubber dinghy is much
more seaworthy as a lifeboat and also
a much safer tender. Best of all is the
inflatable liferaft designed particularly for such situations. Most of
these are self-inflating and can be

ready for use in a matter of seconds.
They can also be pumped up by
hand. The only disadvantage is that
they are expensive, but are still the
best type of lifeboat to have. Even if
they have not been used, it is advisable to have liferafts inspected and
serviced regularly by the makers.

A liferaft of this kind will have a
tent-like cover which should not only
keep out the sea but also protect the
occupants from the weather – the
latter being an important consideration in some situations, when death
from exposure is as big a hazard as
drowning. The raft should also be

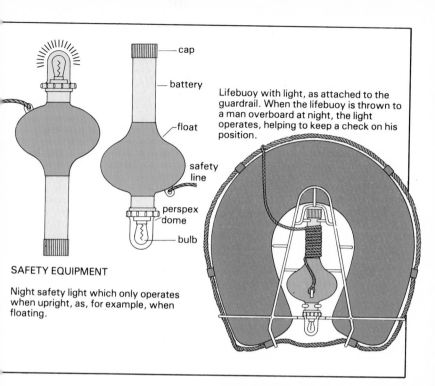

cap

battery

float

safety line

perspex dome

bulb

Lifebuoy with light, as attached to the guardrail. When the lifebuoy is thrown to a man overboard at night, the light operates, helping to keep a check on his position.

SAFETY EQUIPMENT

Night safety light which only operates when upright, as, for example, when floating.

equipped with food and water, a first-aid kit, and distress flares. The parent boat should also have a supply of flares. They should be kept in a watertight container, stowed away in some safe but accessible place.

It must be remembered that the prospect of your getting into so much trouble that you have to set off flares or in the last resort to take to your dinghy or liferaft is a very remote one. In fact *it should never happen*, and almost certainly won't. But you do have to be prepared for all eventualities.

Right: An inflatable liferaft neatly stowed.

151

Man overboard

People are most likely to fall overboard when they are working on deck. It may be that in the excitement of a sail-change in a lively sea, they forget to hold on to something and a wave suddenly shouldering up under the bow throws them off-balance.

Guardrails

To prevent anyone in this situation actually going over the side, most boats have guardrails. These enclose the whole of the deck area and usually consist of a rigid framework round the bows, probably made of stout metal piping, and called a *pulpit* (because that is what it looks like); wire ropes supported by *stanchions* (metal posts) along each side; and

Left: In rough weather, a pulpit, guard-rails and safety harness become vital.

Above: A good example of safety round the bow — the riskiest part of a vessel's deck. Both pulpit and guardrails are sturdy.

Below: A horseshoe-type lifebelt, conveniently placed aft. It is a substantial object, so it should be thrown *near*, not *at* the casualty.

possibly a rear pulpit, known, by sailors' logic, as a *pushpit*.

A pushpit is not as necessary as a pulpit because people do not move around as much at the stern of a boat. Good, strong protection is vital round the bows because most of the work done when under way requires someone to be on the foredeck, and also a boat's motion is always most pronounced up in the bows.

One point to remember is that guardrails must be high enough to do their job properly. Some little boats have very low rails, more for the sake of appearances than anything else. These are positively dangerous because they can act like trip wires and assist rather than hinder your dive over the side.

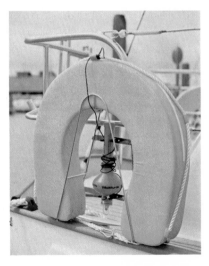

Safety harness

As a rule, when moving about on deck you should have one hand for the boat and one for yourself. You should never relinquish one hand-hold until you have found another. And make sure that the part you hold on to is both strong and rigid. If it is something that swings or bucks or

jerks to the boat's motion, it may tear itself out of your grasp.

When moving about on deck in anything but calm weather, you should always wear a safety harness. There are various models, but they all essentially consist of a belt and a length of line with one or more snap hooks on it. You attach yourself to the

of the line parting, or the part of the boat you are attached to breaking away, is smaller. There is also less chance of personal injury.

Anchor points You must choose very strong anchor points (the part of the boat you attach yourself to). For example, it is not a good idea to snap yourself on to a hand-rail on the cabin top – it is all right for steadying yourself in good weather, but it is only held on by a few wood screws. In practice you should not have any difficulty finding anchor points, because most boats offer plenty of integral parts to hitch on to.

As with a car seat-belt, a safety harness may seem a nuisance and a hindrance to start with, but you will soon get used to wearing one. You will also be able to do your job better because there is no need to worry about your safety. If necessary you will be able to use both hands to do your job, without wishing you had a third to hang on with.

It is obviously more important to wear a safety harness at night than during the day. Some skippers insist on it, whatever the weather conditions. Sometimes it will be advisable for everyone on watch to be harnessed, even those whose duties do not take them around the decks. It is not unknown for a yachtsman to be washed out of the cockpit by a surging sea.

boat by one or other of the snap hooks, according to how much freedom of movement you need for what you have to do. The shorter the length of line you are using the better, since the less distance you travel before you are brought up short by your safety line, the less violent the jerk will be, and therefore the chance

Rescue procedures

There is a set 'man overboard' drill in the case of someone who goes overboard in spite of all these precautions. The person or persons remaining on board must act as follows – and quickly!

A lifebelt, lifejacket, bunk cushion or something that will help to support the casualty should be thrown as near him as possible. If it is a rigid, round or horse-shoe-type, lifebelt, do not throw it *at* him. You might hit him and hurt him, or even knock him out.

Someone on the boat must keep a constant watch on the person in the water. Except on the calmest of days, it is very difficult to spot someone in the sea, and, once you lose sight of him, you may never locate him again. If there is only one person left on board the boat, he must do his utmost to keep the casualty in view while he is carrying out the necessary manoeuvre to pick him up.

Obviously this manoeuvre will be easier if the boat is under power –

MAN OVERBOARD

3. Beat back up to the person.

2. Gybe

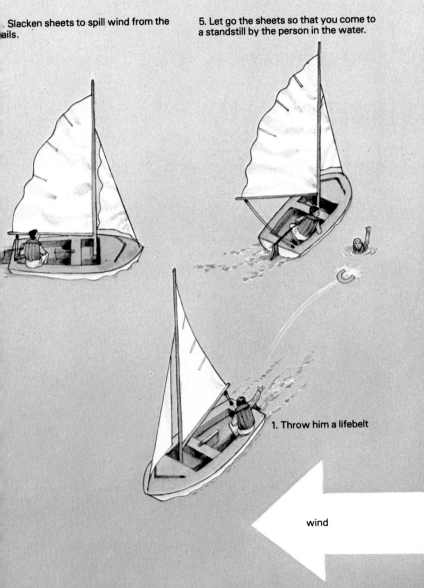

Slacken sheets to spill wind from the
sails.

5. Let go the sheets so that you come to
a standstill by the person in the water.

1. Throw him a lifebelt

wind

157

with her engine running – than it will be if you are sailing. You will have more control, including the ability to 'brake' by going astern as you come up to the casualty, being careful **to keep the propeller away from the person**.

If you are under sail, the whole thing becomes much more of a trial of skill. The procedure is as follows. Whatever the weather is like, and whatever the boat's point of sailing, whether she is running, reaching or beating, **you must gybe.** In other words, you must bring her stern right across the wind, even if, in normal circumstances, this would be an un-seamanlike thing to do. These circumstances are not normal.

The boat has to be gybed because this is the quickest way of getting her into the position down-wind of the person in the water, a position from which she can beat up to him *against* the wind and then reduce speed by heading up further into the wind or slackening off her sheets to spill it out of her sails. One of the greatest dangers involved in trying to pick up someone in the water is of running him down. This may only too easily happen if you approach him down-wind because you will not have any means of immediately slowing down.

1. It is difficult to lift the dead weight of a man-overboard back on board single-handed. He can, however, be lifted aboard by other means.

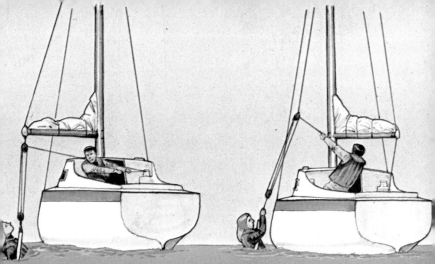

2. Use of the mainsheet and winch.

3. Use of the main halyard or topping lift attached to a winch.

4. Use of the unhanked foresail as a scoop.

5. Use of a portable ladder hooked over the side.

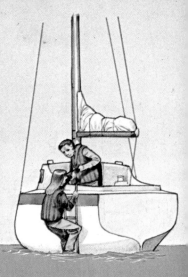

Buoyancy

There are two kinds of buoyancy – the boat's and your own.

It has been mentioned that most dinghies will stay afloat even when full of water. Some will do so because of the materials from which they are constructed, but most will have either air-tight compartments built into them, or inflated bags, called buoyancy bags, held in place in the boat by straps.

A boat which floats when full of water is said to have *positive buoyancy*.

Buoyancy is more important in dinghies than most larger boats because dinghies are more likely to fill with water, most commonly as the result of a capsize. Large boats rarely capsize, which is just as well because most of them have *negative buoyancy*. In other words, if they fill with water they will sink. It is just not practicable for reasons of space to provide them with sufficient buoyancy to compensate for the weight of the ballast keel, engine, and so on. Some very small cabin boats will still float even when full of water, as will some multi-hulls which do not have heavy ballast keels, but these are only the smaller boats.

A dinghy capsize: it need not be a serious matter provided the crew know what to do. The first rule is to stay with the boat, since its buoyancy keeps it floating on the surface of the water and you can hold on to it.

FIRST AID KIT

sterile non-adhesive
dressings

gauze packs — 5 large,
5 small

one triangular bandage
(ie. sling for arm)

cotton wool

one crepe bandage

roll of adhesive plaster

transparent waterproof
tape

rolls of narrow gauze
bandage

assorted safety pins

clinical thermometer

scissors

sea sickness tablets

splints

reflective blanket

antiseptic cream

aspirins

Essential items which should be carried
in a first aid kit for use in emergencies.
Every cruising boat should have a
first aid box.

Fitness

Although physical fitness is important, this does not mean you have to be an athlete to sail. What it does mean is that the better you feel, the more alert and efficient you are likely to be.

It is important to eat properly and to rest before you go on watch. How long any one person remains on watch will depend on factors such as how long a passage you are making, what the weather is like, how many people there are on board. Everyone should spend the same amount of time on watch, and should all have time to relax. Remember that where any kind of sport is concerned, the human body is just as much a part of the equipment as anything else, and needs to be kept in just as good shape.

Remember too that, just as your boat may suffer damage, so may her crew. Every cabin boat should carry a first aid box adequate to cope with any mishaps that may arise, and someone on board should have a basic knowledge of first aid, including artificial respiration.

Don't forget that sea sickness can greatly reduce efficiency. There are a number of effective treatments available in shops for this condition.

Weather

Weather is not of great importance to the dinghy sailor, who is never – or should not be – very far from land. It is of much more concern to people in bigger boats deciding what sort of passage they are going to make, or even whether to put to sea at all.

Broadcast weather forecasts, both the ordinary and the more specialized ones put out for shipping, are reliable, but you should not depend only on these. They cover wide areas, and conditions may be different in your locality.

One instrument every sea-going craft should have is a barometer, to serve as a basic weather guide. A barometer is simply a device for measuring atmospheric pressure. High pressure (what the weather men call a 'high') is indicated by a high reading on the barometer, and means fine weather. A 'low', indicated by a low reading on the barometer, means bad weather.

A slow rise in pressure indicates less wind or rain (or possibly both), a slow fall, more. A rapid rise or fall means a sudden change and a period of generally unsettled conditions.

Right: Section of a typical weather map (synoptic chart) showing symbols commonly used. These can be seen in daily newspapers and at weather stations. Conditions reported at the weather stations are indicated, as shown inset. Particular information is always plotted in the same position around the dot, using symbols.

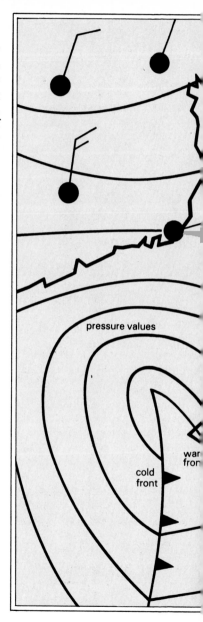

pressure values

warm front

cold front

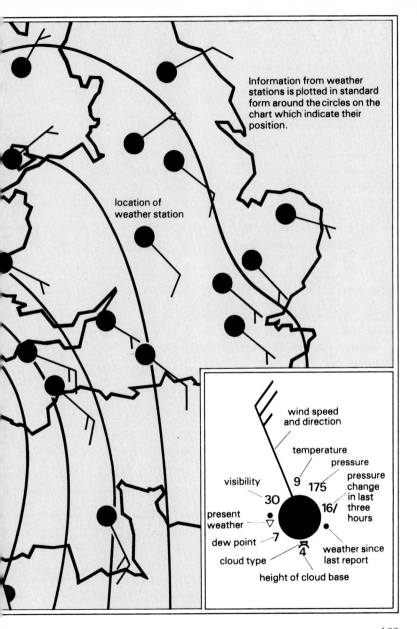

Information from weather stations is plotted in standard form around the circles on the chart which indicate their position.

location of weather station

wind speed and direction

temperature

pressure

visibility

pressure change in last three hours

9

175

30

16/

present weather

dew point

7

weather since last report

cloud type

4

height of cloud base

The sky

We can tell a lot about the weather from cloud formations. There are four main kinds, each with its own special name – cumulus, cirrus, stratus and nimbus.

Cumulus clouds are the ones that look like big white balls of cotton wool or blobs of shaving foam. They are usually sharply outlined against a background of clear blue sky. They are sometimes called 'yachtsman's clouds' because they are a sign of fine weather.

Cirrus is a high, wispy formation. Sometimes called 'mares' tails', it indicates wind. If it spreads across the sky and becomes more regular in pattern, you can expect bad weather.

Stratus is a layer or sheet-type cloud. If it spreads across the sky, rain is on the way and may last some time, although it is unlikely to be heavy.

Nimbus is the grey, ragged stuff a lot of us know only too well. When that covers the sky, it is probably raining already!

These four main types of cloud also occur in various combinations. There is cirro-cumulus, for example, a high formation sometimes called a 'mackerel sky', presumably because somebody saw a likeness in pattern to a mackerel's scales. Patches of cloud may occur in good weather, but if they spread, join up and become regular, conditions are probably going to deteriorate. Cirro-stratus is a thin, whitish cloud which again tends

1

Different cloud types.
1. Cumulus: a sign of fine weather.
2. Cirrus: indicates wind.
3. Cirro-cumulus: the 'mackerel' effect may indicate bad weather.
4. Alto-cumulus: indicates fine weather.
5. Cirro-stratus: usually means bad weather.
6. Fracto-cumulus: unsettled conditions.
7. Cumul-onimbus: the cloud to beware of!

to take on a more definite formation on the approach of bad weather.

Alto-cumulus, or high cumulus, looks like ripples on a sandy beach and is a sign of fine weather. Fracto-cumulus, or broken cumulus, looks like it sounds, and indicates unsettled conditions.

Finally, there is the worst formation of all from the small-boat sailor's point of view. This is cumulo-nimbus, which consists of great piled-up masses of cloud, very dark on the underside. Such clouds indicate heavy rain, possibly with violent squalls of wind and even thunder and lightning.

2

3

4

5

6

7

165

Wind velocities

Weather forecasts include references to the strength of the wind as 'Force so-and-so' – for example, 'South-westerly, Force 5'. This means that the wind will be blowing at a velocity tabulated as Force 5 on the Beaufort Wind Scale, so-named after a distinguished officer in the British Navy, Admiral Sir Francis Beaufort. He was an expert on navigation and meteorology, and drew up the Scale at the beginning of the 19th century. It is still in use today and appears in most 'almanack-style' nautical publications.

Right: Heavy seas breaking over the harbour wall at Mullion Cove, Cornwall, on the far south-west coast of England. The only place for a boat to be in these conditions is in the harbour.

Below: The Beaufort Wind Scale is a useful guide to sailing conditions, including the state of the sea. Crews should always note Beaufort predictions in weather forecasts.

Force	Wind Speed (knots)	Sea Conditions
0	Less than 1	**Calm** No ripples. Any swell is not caused by wind.
1	1 – 3	**Light air** Patches of ripples on surface.
2	4 – 7	**Light breeze** Surface covered by ripples and waves up to 0·3m.
3	8 – 12	**Gentle breeze** Small waves, 0·6 – 0·9m with occasional 'white horses' (breaking waves).
4	13 – 18	**Moderate breeze** Waves up to 1·2 – 1·5m. Numerous 'white horses'.
5	19 – 24	**Fresh breeze** Waves 1·8 – 2·4m with foaming crests. Spray blown from crests.
6	23 – 31	**Strong breeze** Waves 2·4 – 3·7m, crested and streaked with foam. Spray.

7	32 – 38	**Moderate gale** Waves 3·7 – 4·9m with white, foaming crests broken away in gusts.
8	39 – 46	**Fresh gale** Rough and disturbed sea. Waves 6 – 7·6m with seething patches.
9	47 – 54	**Strong gale** Sea covered in white foam. Waves 7·6 – 9·1m. Visibility reduced by spray.
10	55 – 63	**Whole gale** Waves 9·1 – 12·2m. Visibility badly affected.
11	64 – 72	**Storm** Air full of spray. Waves 13·7m. Large vessels may be damaged.
12	73 – 82	**Hurricane** Waves over 13·7m. Damage to large ships and small craft likely to founder (sink).

NB From about Force 6 upwards, yachts' crews are advised to stay at home.

Heavy weather

The good sailor will make an assessment of all the sources of information available to avoid being caught out in really bad conditions, but there are bound to be times when a boat is pressed too hard by the wind.

In such circumstances there are a number of things to do, depending mainly on the boat's course relative to the wind, and whether or not it has an engine.

If it is running down-wind, or on a reach, you can turn into the wind, get the mainsail down, then carry on under jib alone.

If your course is to windward you may have to keep both sails up to preserve the balance of the sail-plan, but reduce the total sail area. In other words, you may have to reef.

Reefing

The basic operation when reefing is to reduce the area of the mainsail. This is done in one of two ways, depending on what kind of reefing gear the boat has. The traditional way is to use *reef points*, which are horizontal rows of short lengths of line hanging from the sail on either side of it. There are usually two or three such rows between the foot of the sail and a third of the way up it, and at each end of each row there is a cringle called a *reef cringle*.

To reef a sail using reef points, the sail must be lowered sufficiently for

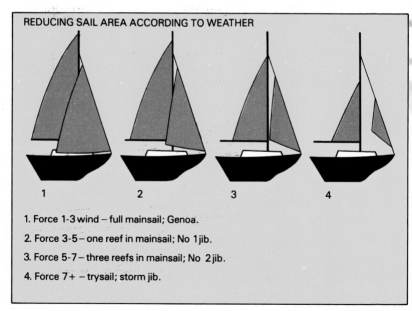

REDUCING SAIL AREA ACCORDING TO WEATHER

1   2   3   4

1. Force 1-3 wind – full mainsail; Genoa.
2. Force 3-5 – one reef in mainsail; No 1 jib.
3. Force 5-7 – three reefs in mainsail; No 2 jib.
4. Force 7+ – trysail; storm jib.

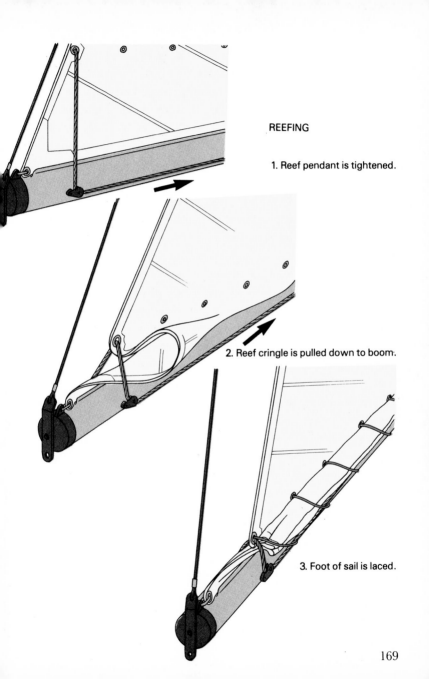

REEFING

1. Reef pendant is tightened.

2. Reef cringle is pulled down to boom.

3. Foot of sail is laced.

the cringles at each end of the row of reef points to be lashed down to the boom. Which row of reef points you use will of course depend on how much you want to reduce your sail area. The tack (forward) cringle should be lashed down first, and the clew (after) cringle pulled aft to get the 'new' foot of the sail taut, just as you do when bending on the sail. The spare part at the bottom is then gathered up and secured by tying each pair of reef points round the sail using a reef knot (see page 201). Note that the reef points should be tied round the sail, not round the boom. The only thing that now remains is to set up the new luff as taut as you can get it.

To take out (shake out) a reef, all you have to do is untie the reef points and cringle lashings, then set up the sail on the halyard again.

Roller reefing Most modern boats have a much simpler method of reefing, called roller-reefing. No reef points are required for this. A roller-reefing mainsail has a boom which can be rotated either by a mechanism, or, in the case of some very small boats, by hand. To reef, you merely slack off on the halyard and roll the sail round the boom like a roller blind, while shaking out a reef is simply a reversal of this procedure. You can reduce the area of the sail as much as you want by taking as many rolls round the boom as are required.

Nowadays roller-reefing has almost completely replaced the old points method, although the latter still has its champions (as do so many traditional things about sailing craft). They think it is more nautical, and, from a practical point of view, that a rotating boom is just one more mechanical contraption that may go wrong.

Jibs On small boats it is usually sufficient to reef the mainsail, leaving

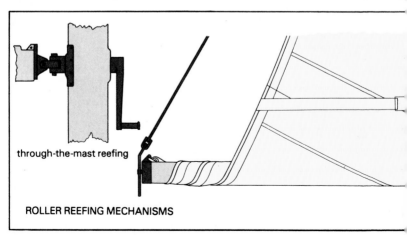

through-the-mast reefing

ROLLER REEFING MECHANISMS

170

he jib alone. If it should be necessary
o reduce the area of sail in front of the
mast, this is nearly always done by
changing the jib for a smaller one,
though on some older boats you may
see jibs with reef-points.

You may also occasionally come
across a roller-reefing jib, which is the
simplest thing in the world to use. It is
usually operated by a line and drum
at the foot of the luff. Slack off whichever jib sheet is in use, pull in the slack
on the luff drum, and the sail will roll
itself up round its luff wire like a
spring-loaded blind. To unfurl it
again, release the drum line and pull
in the jib sheet to re-trim the sail. The
advantage of this is that you can vary
the area of the sail without leaving
the cockpit. The disadvantage is that
the mechanism required is rather
cumbersome, giving the jib a thick
luff which must detract from the
boat's performance.

A well-equipped sea-going craft

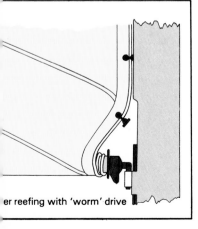

er reefing with 'worm' drive

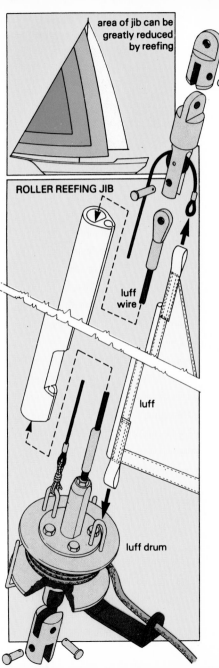

area of jib can be
greatly reduced
by reefing

ROLLER REEFING JIB

luff
wire

luff

luff drum

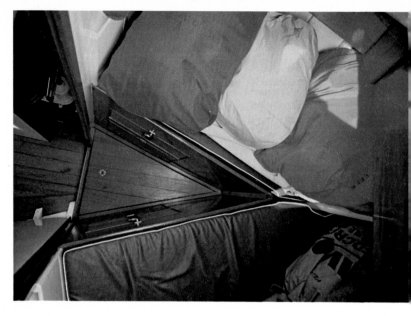

will have three jibs of diminishing sizes, known respectively as 'No. 1', 'No. 2', and 'No. 3' jibs. An ocean-voyager may also have two very small, very tough triangles, namely a *storm jib* and a *storm trysail,* the latter being set in place of the mainsail.

When not in use, sails should be stowed in sail bags. Each should have its own bag, which should be clearly marked as to its contents.

Safety precautions Reefing at sea is almost always done in rough or at least lively weather. This is one occasion, then, when safety harness *must* be worn. With most boats, it will also be necessary to get the boom as far inboard as possible to reef, and the engine, if there is one, can be used to head the boat directly into the wind.

You must be able to find the right sail straight away. Each of them should have its own clearly-marked bag to avoid confusion.

In fact an engine can be very useful in bad weather, though one should always keep some sail up as well, in case the machinery fails. The ordinary boat's engine is called an auxiliary which means 'a help', and that is what it should be.

If, just before the start of a trip, the weather is reasonable but looks as though it is going to get worse, you might be wise to reef before you start off. You will be able to do it much more easily in the shelter of an anchorage or harbour, and you can always shake it out if the weather does not turn out to be as bad as expected

Boat Maintenance

Maintenance is a vital aspect of sailing from the point of view of both satisfaction and safety. If your boat is not in tip-top shape, she will not sail as well as she should and you will not get the satisfaction you should out of sailing her. If a shroud or your anchor cable parts (breaks), or your engine will not start, you could be in danger.

Up to a point, maintenance will depend on what sort of boat you have. If she is a dinghy which is towed to and from home, you will be able to work on her when you feel like it. A larger boat will probably have to stay out in her sailing area, and you can work on her there. Some people pay boatyards to look after their boats for them.

A lot of people, especially dinghy owners, sail all the year round, but usually it is a sport to be done during the better months of the year. For most people the sailing season starts some time during the spring and goes through to the late summer or autumn. It will be preceded by a period of *fitting out*, which means getting the boat ready for the season, and followed by *laying up* – putting the boat away for the winter period when you will not be using her.

There are always jobs to be done for the sake of safety and performance.

Laying up

A mudberth. A boat left for the winter in such conditions must be moored securely and visited as often as possible.

If you cannot tow your boat home, there are various ways in which she can be laid up. She can be left afloat, but this has a number of disadvantages. It means she will be exposed to the winter weather, and you will have to visit her from time to time to make sure she has not broken adrift and that she is not taking in water – in short, that she is still where she ought to be, and still afloat!

In suitable areas a boat can be left in a mudberth, which is simply an indentation in the shore – usually muddy, hence the name. The advan-

tages of this over leaving a boat lying off (afloat) is that access, which will usually be by means of a gangplank, is a great deal easier, and the boat will normally be more secure. There may still be some danger of her breaking adrift, and driving ashore, or filling with water.

The majority of boats left in their sailing areas are laid up ashore – in other words on dry land – either out-of-doors or in a boatshed. This makes access easier still, and you do not have to worry about moorings or leaks.

The advantage of laying up a boat in a shed is that you can carry out most refitting work at any time, irrespective of the weather. For example, you can paint the outside of the hull while people with boats out in the open are crouching in their cabins with paintbrushes at the ready, waiting for the rain to stop.

The only real disadvantage about laying up under cover is that the roof over your head will probably be the boatyard's and it will cost you more to keep your boat there than it would in the same boatyard out in the open. In any case, most boatyards have only very limited under-cover space, so the great majority of boats have to be laid up outside.

Boats with retractable or twin bilge keels will sit quite happily on dry land, perhaps with a little packing material to stabilize them completely. So also will multi-hulled craft (catamarans and trimarans).

Boats with central, fixed keels of any appreciable depth are more of a problem. A few have sturdy posts called 'legs' which can be bolted on to the hull half-way along its length, one on either side, but this method of support is, generally speaking, only temporary and confined to older craft. The most common procedure is to prop the boat up with a number of heavy baulks of wood on either side sloping up from the ground to meet the curve of the hull at right-angles. These baulks are called *shores,* which is why a boat thus supported is said to be shored up. Shoring up a boat of any size is a skilled and potentially dangerous job which is best left to a boatyard.

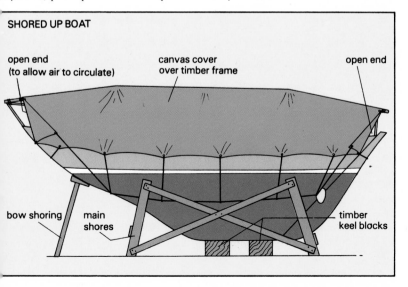

SHORED UP BOAT

open end
(to allow air to circulate)

canvas cover
over timber frame

open end

bow shoring

main
shores

timber
keel blocks

Once you have laid up your boat, you will have several months to work on her. If she is a dinghy, you will probably be able to do everything yourself, especially if you have her laid up at home. If you have a larger boat which you are leaving in the care of a boatyard, you can still work on her yourself. A good boatyard will not mind, especially if you are buying at least some of your materials from them anyway. If you need to call in another professional for a specialized job, you should first seek the permission of the yard owner. If you want the yard to do certain jobs for you, let them know in good time because the yard may have a last minute rush of work it cannot cope with, and you will be late getting into the water.

Having work done by a boatyard is expensive. But with larger boats there are a couple of jobs that yards will almost certainly have to do. One of these jobs is getting the boat out of

he water at the end of the season, and he other is putting her back in at the beginning of the next. This expenditure is a good example of what makes such a difference in cost between big boat and dinghy sailing.

As far as other jobs are concerned, ou should make it a rule to let the ard do anything that may affect the afety of the boat which you are not ure you can manage efficiently yourelf.

You should get down to your boat as often as you can during the winter. You may go only to check that she is still safe and sound, but no doubt there will be jobs you can do while you are there. If it is a nice day, take the cover off the boat and open her right up. A good dose of fresh air, and, if you are lucky, some sunshine, will do a lot to keep her 'sweet'.

Cleaning off a boat below the waterline. In the old days this meant using a bucket and scrubbing brush. Nowadays a high-pressure hose will do most of the job.

De-rigging

When a boat is laid up, she should be de-rigged and her mast or masts unstepped (taken out). The rigging, both standing and running, must be carefully inspected, and any unsatisfactory items repaired or replaced. This is a job which, equally important in dinghies and large craft, can be done at leisure during the laid-up period, either at the boa or at home.

Masts must be kept somewhere with equal support along their whole length to avoid any damaging stresses after being unstepped.

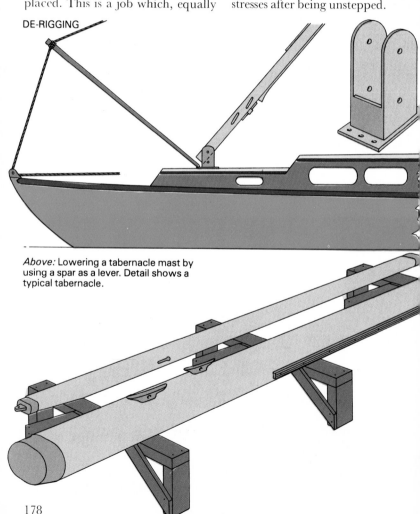

DE-RIGGING

Above: Lowering a tabernacle mast by using a spar as a lever. Detail shows a typical tabernacle.

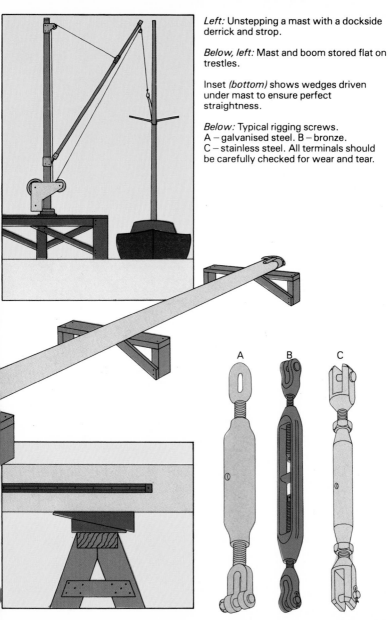

Left: Unstepping a mast with a dockside derrick and strop.

Below, left: Mast and boom stored flat on trestles.

Inset *(bottom)* shows wedges driven under mast to ensure perfect straightness.

Below: Typical rigging screws.
A – galvanised steel. B – bronze.
C – stainless steel. All terminals should be carefully checked for wear and tear.

A   B   C

Damp

The great enemy of boats when they are laid up is damp (this applies even to boats laid up under cover, although to a lesser degree). For this reason anything liable to be affected in this way must be removed, especially clothing and bedding. In fact, by the end of the season almost everything is likely to suffer from the damp, so it is a good idea to clear out all portable items and take them home to be cleaned.

Once the rigging has been removed and the mast unstepped (possibly the guard rails will have been removed as well), a cover must be rigged over the whole length of any boat left in the open. Some boats have specially 'tailored' boat covers, but a great many make do with a weatherproof rectangular sheet of some sort, either of plastic or canvas material. The cover should be stretched over a ridge-pole running the whole length of the boat, like the roof of a ridge tent, and should be secured by 'guy ropes' to a rope running round the boat below its maximum girth. The 'tent' should be left

open at both ends to allow air to pass through. For the same reason all floorboards should be lifted and all locker doors left open.

The point of all this is to prevent pockets of damp air forming, which in a wooden boat can lead to serious hull weakness. Even in a boat with a GRP hull, there are likely to be some wooden parts, and these could suffer from damp. At the least, a boat which has been left inadequately ventilated will develop a musty smell which will persist for a surprisingly long time after the start of the next season.

It is advisable to make an inventory of what you take off the boat, to ensure that everything comes back on board again in due course. Items which are not easily recognizable – rigging wires for example – should be given identifying labels. If you are leaving things at a boatyard, everything should also carry the name of the boat and its owner.

Dinghies laid up well out of the water with covers. Although this is satisfactory in summer, the boats would be likely to suffer from damp in winter.

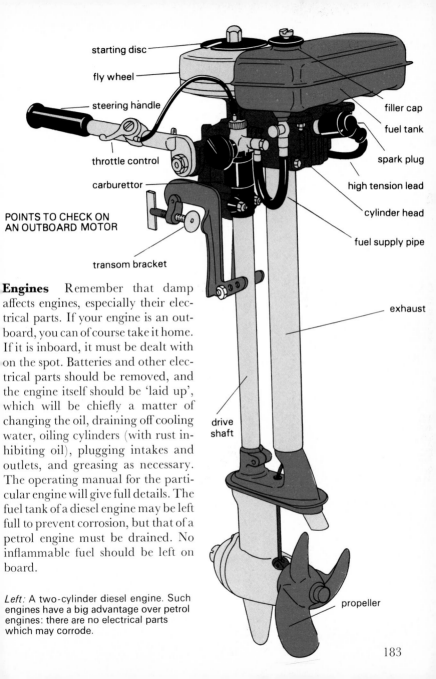

starting disc

fly wheel

steering handle

throttle control

carburettor

**POINTS TO CHECK ON
AN OUTBOARD MOTOR**

transom bracket

filler cap

fuel tank

spark plug

high tension lead

cylinder head

fuel supply pipe

exhaust

drive
shaft

propeller

Engines Remember that damp affects engines, especially their electrical parts. If your engine is an outboard, you can of course take it home. If it is inboard, it must be dealt with on the spot. Batteries and other electrical parts should be removed, and the engine itself should be 'laid up', which will be chiefly a matter of changing the oil, draining off cooling water, oiling cylinders (with rust inhibiting oil), plugging intakes and outlets, and greasing as necessary. The operating manual for the particular engine will give full details. The fuel tank of a diesel engine may be left full to prevent corrosion, but that of a petrol engine must be drained. No inflammable fuel should be left on board.

Left: A two-cylinder diesel engine. Such engines have a big advantage over petrol engines: there are no electrical parts which may corrode.

General maintenance

Cleaning When your boat comes out of the water at the end of the season, she will probably have a dirty bottom; in other words, she may have growths of weeds and barnacles on and below the waterline. The first job to be done, perhaps while she is still on the slipway, is to scrub or scrape her clean; the process will probably require both actions.

It will make life a lot easier and you will get better results if you do your bigger jobs in a sensible sequence. Washing down the inside of the hull and cleaning out the bilges, for example, is a chore it is hard to feel enthusiastic about, and you may be tempted to put it off and get on with something more interesting. But this is a job that should be undertaken as soon as the boat is laid up, partly to get it out of the way, and partly, again, to make the boat wholesome.

VIEW OF A BUSY BOAT YARD

Sails It is a good idea to make lists of what you have to do during the laid-up period. One job you would be wise to do early on is inspection of your sails. These are expensive, and will repay careful looking-after. You should either have them washed (if there is a sail-maker near, he will do it for you), or, if they are not too big, you can wash them yourself. You should inspect them for wear and tear, and either repair the damage yourself or get it done professionally as soon as possible. Sail-makers are busy people, and if you leave it too long you may find yourself at the end of a queue and missing part of the next year's sailing season.

Not for a dinghy! Here, in the making, is the mainsail of the yacht Britannia, which belonged to King George V of Britain. This was the largest sail loft in Europe.

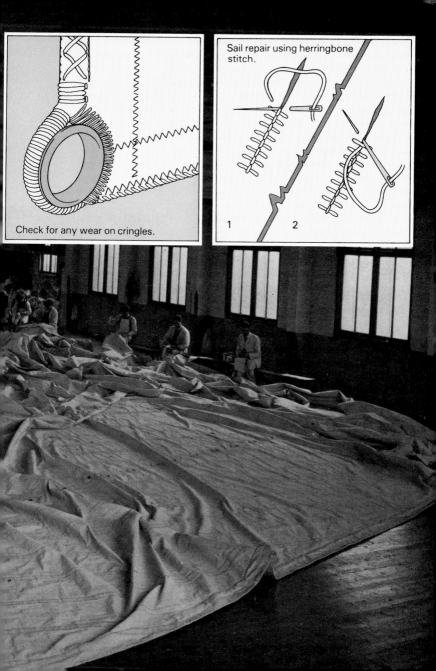

Check for any wear on cringles.

Sail repair using herringbone stitch.

1 2

Painting and varnishing Treating the hull is left until the spring, so that the boat will look really sparkling when she goes into the water again. Outside varnishing, which should be done on a warm, windless day, is similarly another task to be left until spring.

The procedure for painting or varnishing the hull will depend on what it is made of, and also on what sort of boat you have. With a wooden hull you will be following much the same procedure as for any wood exposed to the weather – as, for example, the outside of your front door at home – although you will naturally get the best results if you use good quality marine products. It will be a matter of rubbing down, 'making good' by filling gaps and holes, and applying as many undercoats as you consider necessary, with a gloss paint over that – preferably one of the very durable polyurethane paints, or yacht enamel. GRP hulls require different treatment which includes the sealing of abrasions with gel coat and the filling of cavities with epoxy stopping. If the hull is very badly scuffed, it can

PROCEDURE FOR PAINTING

1. Scrape off the old paint.

2. Sand-down the surface.

3. Rub off the dust.

4. Apply the paint.

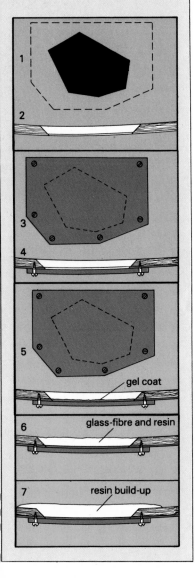

REPAIR TO A DAMAGED GRP BOAT

1

2

3

4

5

gel coat

6

glass-fibre and resin

7

resin build-up

Left: When hole is accessible from both sides, cut away jagged edges. Apply former (1) to cover hole. Cut skin thickness back at an angle (2). Screw former into place (3 and 4). Apply gel coat to inside of former and leave to harden (5). Apply layers of glass-fibre and resin (6). Build up resin around the damaged area (7), and rub down.

Below: When damage cannot be reached from both sides, push resin-covered metal mesh patch through hole (A) and secure with wire (B). When resin has hardened, build up layers of resin and glass-fibre (C).

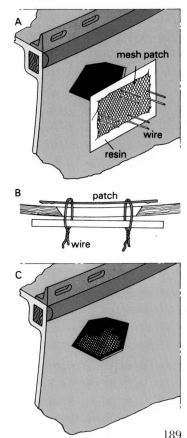

A

mesh patch

wire

resin

B

patch

wire

C

be painted in the same way as a wooden hull. (This may all sound very technical, but instructions are readily available and easy to follow.)

Some dinghies have varnished hulls and look very nice. You may also occasionally see a larger boat finished in this way, but not many, because usually paint is easier to apply, and presents a better appearance. The traditional and most common colour for yacht hulls continues to be white.

Below: Scraping the topsides of a wooden racing yacht before varnishing. *Bottom:* Varnishing the forehatch – a job for a warm, still day. Nothing looks smarter than a bit of 'brightwork'!

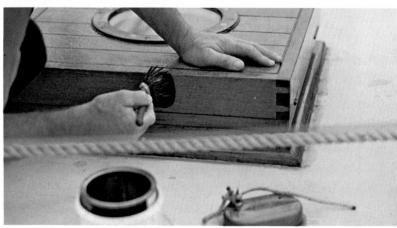

Fitting out

A racing yacht which has been taken out of the water for mid-season cleaning. It is being checked for any damage.

The process of getting a boat ready for the new season can be either a pleasure or a chore according to what is involved, how you go about it, and what you did when laying up the previous autumn. If you did the latter properly and have attended to all the jobs you reasonably could during the winter, then fitting out will be a pleasure, and an exciting business too. You will soon be afloat again! If, on the other hand, you have left everything to the last moment, you are likely to find yourself involved in a mad scramble, in the course of which some things will be forgotten.

Ideally, fitting out should be like a film of laying up run backwards. Everything taken off the boat should come back on board in reverse order. This is when you find out that it is useful to have labelled everything you took off the boat – you should know where to put each stay, for example.

One of the last jobs to be done on larger boats is the application of antifouling paint below the water-line. This is done to discourage marine growths. If your boat has been lying

in a mudberth, you will have to get her out and on to a slipway or some kind of hard standing and clean off her bottom, then apply the paint. Applying anti-fouling is always left until just before launching the boat to preserve its protective strength: it should not be exposed to the air for longer than is absolutely necessary.

This does not apply to dinghies, which can be scrubbed off at any time. Far from applying anti-fouling, the owner of a racing dinghy is much more likely to be found lovingly polishing the bottom of his boat to make her slip through the water just that little bit quicker.

Mid-season maintenance

Maintenance during the season can be divided into two categories – regular jobs, and those which must be done as and when necessary. For example, washing down decks on a cruising boat should be a daily chore, while renewing a halyard will be a 'one-off'.

A job which will probably have to be done at least once if you are sailing a larger boat on the sea will be renewing the anti-fouling, because, while these compounds discourage marine growths, they will not prevent them completely, and a build-up will materially affect a boat's speed. If you want to get the best out of your boat, therefore, you may need to scrub the bottom and apply a fresh coat of anti-fouling somewhere around the middle of the season, or perhaps more often than that. Some racing yacht crews do so every few weeks, some before every race.

This operation requires getting the boat out of the water, either by having her slipped (hauled up a slipway by a boatyard), which is expensive, or alternatively by beaching her at a suitable spot at high water, and then

working on her after the tide has receded. If a boat has a central fixed keel, it may take two tides to do the job, since she will have to be laid over first to one side, then the other. Alternatively, the boat can be tied up alongside a harbour wall or something similar, where she will be left high and dry at low water, but again, alongside a wall, you will probably only be able to do one side at a time. A great improvement on this are the detached 'scrubbing posts' which most harbours and some sailing clubs have set up, which you can tie up to, and where you can do both sides on the one tide.

Provided you have fitted out properly, it is unlikely you will have a great deal to do during the sailing season itself. It is important, however, that everything on a boat should be kept clean and tidy. Articles left lying around on deck, or not properly stowed away, can cause accidents.

Ropes and Ropework

A mooring line fastened round a cleat. Ropes should always be stowed neatly in the interests of safety.

Rope is an essential aboard boats, and especially sailing boats. The term 'rope' is used not only for the usual kind (made of hemp, sisal or synthetic material), but also for the wires used for standing rigging (shrouds and stays). Wire rope is also commonly used for halyards because it has less give than ordinary rope, making it possible to get a really taut luff which is all-important in windward sailing. Wire halyards, unless connected directly to a winch, usually have rope tails (a short length of rope spliced on to the lower ends of the halyards) by which they can be made fast; it would be impossible to secure a wire rope round a cleat.

Jib sheets are seldom made of wire, but are rope, nowadays usually a soft, braided rope for the whole of their length. The mainsheet, because it has to run through a block, or series of blocks, is always soft, plaited rope. Plaited rope is very flexible, easy to handle, and seldom kinks, so it is ideal as a sail controlling rope.

The ropes used for mooring are usually the ordinary kind. Mooring ropes are called *warps*, and a cabin boat should carry a number of them of adequate length for any mooring. For example, if you want to make fast alongside a quay or another boat, you will need four warps to do the job properly, namely, a bow and a stern rope to hold her in, and two 'springs' put out diagonally to prevent her moving ahead or astern. The tails of the springs are often used as 'breast' ropes to an adjacent boat for extra security in mooring.

Warps are also used for towing and have all sorts of other general-purpose uses as well, such as tying down loose objects.

This array of halyards would confuse an inexperienced sailor, but they are arranged in an orderly fashion.

Natural and synthetic ropes

Until comparatively recently, all 'ordinary' ropes were made of natural materials such as hemp and sisal, both of which are fibrous plants. Then, about 50 years ago, ropes made of synthetic fibres began to make their appearance. These have rapidly become more and more popular, but there are still plenty of the other kind around.

What are the advantages and disadvantages of the two kinds of rope? The score comes out almost wholly in favour of the synthetics. They are not subject to the rot and mildew which attack natural fibre ropes if they are left wet for any length of time, and they do not become stiff and hard to handle when wet, as do some natural fibre ropes, notably hemp. In fact even long-term immersion does not affect synthetic ropes at all. Also, size for size, they are very much stronger. About the only point against them is that synthetic ropes are more expensive.

Size of rope

It is important to use rope not only of sufficient strength but also the right thickness for a particular job, and here a minor disadvantage of synthetic ropes becomes apparent. Since they are so much stronger, they can be a lot thinner than a natural fibre rope adequate to perform the same function, but this can be a drawback. For example, synthetic jib-sheets on a

dinghy might be so thin that they would cut the hands of the crew member using them. Synthetic rope of about the same diameter as natural fibre rope would have to be used, which would not only be much too strong for the job, which does not matter, but also more expensive, which does!

It is also important that ropes which pass through blocks are the right size for those blocks, particularly that they are not too thin. Too thin a rope may come off the *sheave* (the wheel) and jam between the sheave and the *shell* (the casing) of the block. If that happens when you are trying to lower a sail, you could find yourself in not only a frustrating but a dangerous situation.

You are less likely to try to use too thick a rope for the block it is required to pass through. If you do, it will certainly jam.

In either case, whether a rope is too thick or too thin, it will wear out more quickly than will one of the right size.

Laid and plaited rope

Rope is said to be 'laid' or 'plaited' (or sometimes 'braided') according to the way it is made. Of the two kinds, laid rope is by far the most common and the most useful except

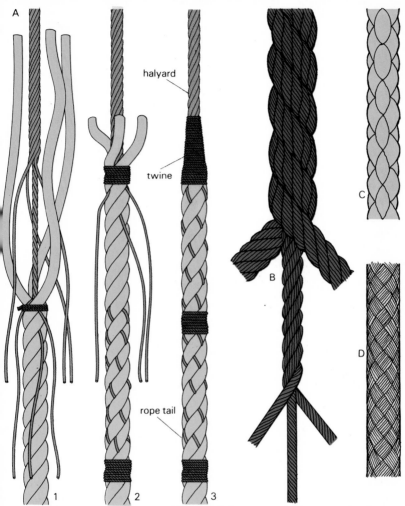

A

halyard

twine

rope tail

1   2   3

B

C

D

for specialized uses such as making sheets. Plaited rope is less strong and difficult to splice (join together).

The process of making laid rope involves: (1) spinning the basic fibre into *yarns* twisted in one direction; (2) twisting, or 'laying' (hence the name

of the process) the yarns in the op-posite direction to form *strands*; (3) twisting the strands in the opposite direction again, to form the rope.

Most laid ropes have three strands, and these can easily be separated for splicing.

Whipping

The ends of laid ropes will fray unless something is done to prevent it. In synthetic ropes, all that is necessary is to hold the end in a flame for a short time, which will make it melt and congeal into a solid blob when it cools.

The ends of natural-fibre ropes are prevented from fraying by whipping, which means binding them with twine. Whipping can be done in a number of ways. The seaman's, or ordinary, whipping is the simplest. To do this, you lay a loop of twine along the end of the rope, make a number of tight turns round the rope, pass the free end through the loop

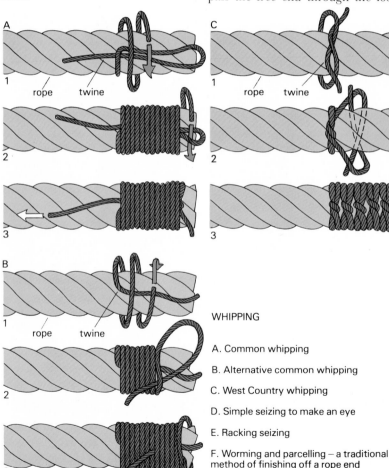

WHIPPING

A. Common whipping

B. Alternative common whipping

C. West Country whipping

D. Simple seizing to make an eye

E. Racking seizing

F. Worming and parcelling – a traditional method of finishing off a rope end and pull the loop through under the turns, finishing off by cutting off the protruding ends. Unfortunately this kind of whipping tends to come off rather easily.

An improvement is what is known as an American whipping, which is much the same as seaman's whipping, but finished off more securely. Better still is a whipping which orig-inated on the west coast of Britain and known appropriately as West Country whipping. This involves making half-knots on opposite sides of the rope at every turn. Best of all is the sailmaker's whipping, in which the twine is not only bound round the rope but worked in between the strands as well and completed with a reef knot.

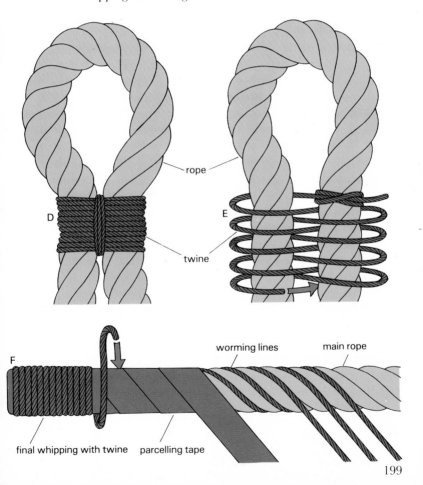

D — rope — twine

E

F — final whipping with twine — parcelling tape — worming lines — main rope

Knots

Many people unfamiliar with sailing think a wide knowledge of knots is required. This is not the case. It is necessary to know only a few.

Overhand knot
This is the simplest of all knots, the one most frequently used for tying anything. All you do is make an overhand loop, pass the end up through the loop and pull tight.

One of the essential requirements of a nautical knot is that it must be easy to untie. The overhand knot does not meet this requirement, as anyone who has ever struggled to undo the string round a parcel will appreciate. But this knot does have a function as a part of other knots.

Bowline
The bowline, used to form an 'eye' in the end of a rope, is one of the most useful of all knots aboard a boat. The eye can be any size, and it will not slip up the rope the way a slipknot does, so the knot will never jam hard round anything.

A bowline may be used for mooring simply by dropping it over a mooring post. A tip here, though. If

there is another vessel already moored to the post in the same way, pass your bowline up through the other one before dropping it over the post. Then either can be lifted off without removing the other.

There are various kinds of bowline – the running bowline, double bowline, bowline on a bight – but these are used for specialized purposes. The simple bowline is the only one that really matters to the ordinary small-boat sailor.

Sheet bend
This knot is used for joining two ropes together. It is not essential because the job can be done by knots already discussed, such as the reef knot, or even two bowlines, one passing through the other.

The sheet bend's real usefulness is for joining two ropes of different thicknesses. This cannot be done effectively by a reef knot, and two bowlines would be unnecessarily complicated and untidy.

Fisherman's knot

This is a very good knot for joining two very thin lines together. It is unsuitable for large calibre ropes, because it will be difficult or impossible, depending on diameter and type, to tie tight overhand knots in such ropes. Also, the resultant fisherman's knot, even if you did manage to achieve it, would be a large lump.

FISHERMAN'S KNOT

REEF KNOT (to join two ropes)

FIGURE-OF-EIGHT KNOT (to stop a rope running out through a block)

Hitches

A hitch is used for 'hitching on to' something, usually temporarily, as, for example, when tying up your dinghy tender to a quay or jetty while you go ashore for stores during a cruise.

Half-hitch

The simplest hitch of all is called a half-hitch, because it is usually only the first stage of what you are going to do. It consists of passing the end of the rope round the object you are hitching to and tying an overhand knot.

The trouble with a simple half-hitch is that it can easily come undone. It is usually backed up, therefore, by another overhand knot. This gives you a second half-hitch, and if this is pushed up close to the first, the knot will be secure.

ROUND TURN AND TWO HALF HITCHES

(to stop a rope slipping)

CLOVE HITCH

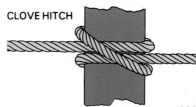

There are various other kinds of hitch, but the foregoing are the most useful to the small-boat sailor, and all that are needed.

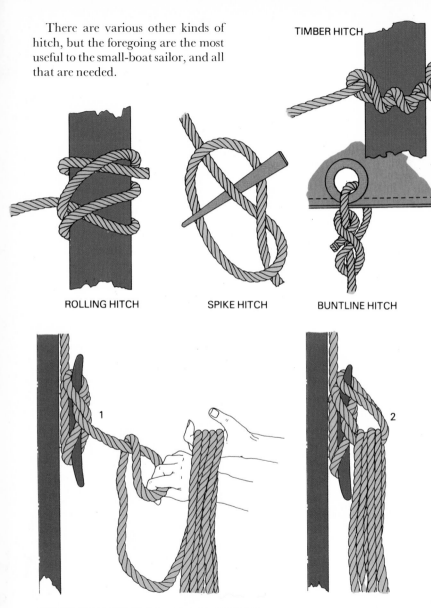

TIMBER HITCH

ROLLING HITCH

SPIKE HITCH

BUNTLINE HITCH

SECURING A HALYARD FALL TO A MAST CLEAT

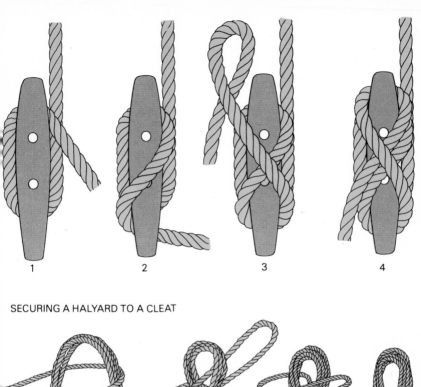

SECURING A HALYARD TO A CLEAT

CAPSIZING OR COILING A LENGTH OF ROPE

Splices

The small-boat sailor ought to know how to make two kinds of splice: an ordinary splice and an eye splice.

Both are made by unlaying the strands of the rope for a short distance from the end and tucking them in between the strands of the other rope or the same rope.

The ordinary splice is used to join two lengths of rope together. The eye splice is used to make a permanent *eye* or loop at the end of a rope. It is also possible to back-splice a rope instead of whipping it or exposing it to heat, to prevent it fraying, but this is only a rather clumsy alternative, and so is not included here.

Ordinary splice

Note Because it has a lower friction-coefficient (that is, it is more slippery) a synthetic rope needs at least one extra full tuck all round for a short splice to have the same holding power as one made in natural fibre rope. If the rope is likely to come under any appreciable strain, it might therefore be advisable to unlay it a little further, perhaps 12 instead of 10 times

Below: Ordinary splice.

1. Separate the strands at the ends of the two ropes and marry each strand

between two strands of the other rope.

2. Tuck the middle strand over an outer strand, under the next and pull it through

ORDINARY SPLICE

EYE SPLICE

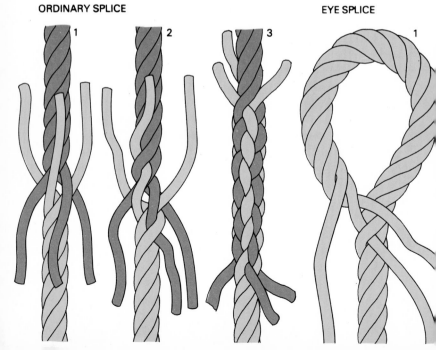

he diameter, before commencing the
ucking process.

Because the splice increases the
hickness of the rope at that point a
ope with a short splice cannot be
sed to run through a block. If a
oined rope is to be employed for this
urpose, a longer splice must be
nade. If a long splice is done pro-
erly, it will not increase the thick-
ess of the rope at all. It should even
e difficult to detect where the join
as been made.

When finished, splices should be
vell stretched and rolled to settle
hem down and smooth them out.

The most effective way of doing the
latter is to roll them underfoot.

Eye splice

An eye splice is intended to be permanent. It is therefore likely to be
subject to much wear, and for this
reason it is usually made round a
concave-grooved metal shape called
a *thimble*.

These are only the essentials of
small-boat ropework. There are
many more bends, hitches, and knots
which you can learn, if you so wish,
from one of the books specifically on
ropework.

hen tuck over and under again.

. Continue this with each strand until all
he unlaid length has been used.

Below, left to right: Eye splice.

Same method as ordinary splice, but
tuck unlaid strands into the same rope.

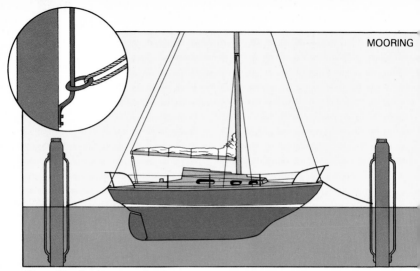

Above: Mooring between piles. Inset shows the sliding iron ring through which the mooring line can be slipped.
Below, left: Mooring alongside a jetty with bow and stern lines (A and B) and springs (C and D).

Below, right: When you come ashore in a tender and other boats are already tied up, slip your painter up through the other lines for easy removal.

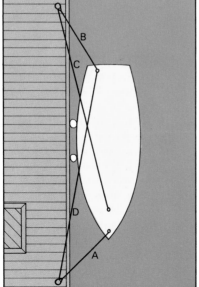

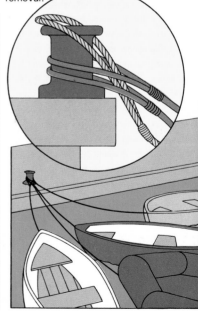

When launching from a trailer, the dinghy should be tied at the bow so that as it floats, the line can be taken ashore.

ROWING

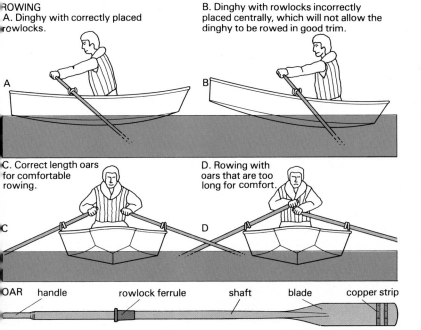

A. Dinghy with correctly placed rowlocks.

B. Dinghy with rowlocks incorrectly placed centrally, which will not allow the dinghy to be rowed in good trim.

A

B

C. Correct length oars for comfortable rowing.

D. Rowing with oars that are too long for comfort.

C

D

OAR   handle   rowlock ferrule   shaft   blade   copper strip

Types of Sailing Craft

Note: A boat's type can be identified by the top-most symbol on its mainsail.

Above, left: International Optimist — ideal beginner's boat, sailed only by people under the age of 15. L.O.A. — 2.3m: beam — 1.13m: weight — 35kg: rig — una spritsail: sail area — 3.25sq.m: crew — 1.

Above: Mirror — all-purpose family cruising dinghy. L.O.A. — 3.9m: beam — 1.58m: weight — 59kg: rig — gunter sloop: sail area — 8.8sq.m: crew — 2.

Left: The Minisail has an overall length of less than 4m. It has an una Bermudan rig and is basically a sailing surfboard.

Above, right: Topper – an ideal family boat, designed for off-the-beach launching. L.O.A. – 3.4m: beam – 1.17m: weight – 38.1kg: rig – una Bermudan: sail area – 5.2sq.m: crew – 1 or 2.

Above: Laser M – intended for single-handed racing and as a family boat. L.O.A. – 4.23m: beam – 1.37m: weight – 58.96kg: rig – una Bermudan: sail area – 5.57sq.m: crew – 1.

Right: A windsurfer. Windsurfing is an increasingly popular sport throughout the world.

Above, left: National Firefly – very popular boat, especially for team racing. L.O.A. – 3.66m: beam – 1.42m: weight – 99.79kg: rig – Bermudan sloop: sail area – 8.36sq.m: crew – 2.

Above: International Enterprise – primarily a racing dinghy, but also used for cruising. L.O.A. – 4.04m: weight – 90.26kg: rig – Bermudan sloop: sail area – 10.5sq.m.: crew – 2.

Left: Conway One-design – a traditional dinghy or day boat, of about 5m length. There are many minor classes of boat which are found mainly in one particular locality.

Above, right: International Fourteen – the class around which modern dinghy sailing developed. L.O.A. – 4.27m: beam – 1.68m: weight – 102kg: rig – Bermudan sloop: sail area – 11.61m: crew – 2.

Above: National Solo – ideal for both young and older helmsmen, it is also claimed to be one of the easiest of all dinghies to right and sail on after a capsize. L.O.A. – 3.78m: beam – 1.55m: weight – 70kg: rig – una Bermudan: sail area – 8.36sq.m: crew – 1.

Right: International 470, with a length of 4.7m, is ideal for highly competitive performance racing.

Above, left: International Flying Dutchman – claimed to be the fastest two-man dinghy in the world, it is not suitable for beginners. L.O.A. – 6.05m: beam – 1.72m: weight – 165.11kg: rig – Bermudan sloop: sail area – 18.58sq.m.: crew – 2.

Above: International 5-0-5 – another fast two-man dinghy, extremely efficient but requires a good helmsman. L.O.A. – 5.05m: beam – 1.88m: weight – 127kg: rig – Bermudan sloop: sail area – 14.5sq.m: crew – 2.

Left: International Fireball is particularly popular in countries with warm climates since in rough conditions she can be a cold, wet boat. Just under 5m long, she is particularly easy for amateurs to build.

Above, right: International Tornado – an extremely fast catamaran. L.O.A. – 6.1m: beam – 3.05m: weight – 125.19kg: rig – Bermudan sloop: sail area – 21.83sq.m: crew – 2.

Above: Wayfarer – mostly used as a family cruising dinghy, very stable and therefore ideal for beginners. L.O.A. – 4.83m: beam – 2.44m: weight – 166kg: rig – Bermudan sloop: sail area – 8.8sq.m: crew – 2.

Right: National Flying Fifteen – a stable boat with a fixed keel and a length of just over 6m.

Above, left: Maxi 68, a cruising boat with a length of 7m.

Above: Moody 39, a four cabin, 8/9 berth cruising boat with a length of 11.73m and a beam of 4.06m.

Left: A typical cruising catamaran with the cabin built between the two hulls.

Above, right: Fisher 34, a heavy displacement cruising yacht with a length of 10.36m.

Above: Westerly W36, a three-cabin cruising boat with a length of 10.9m and beam of 3.4m.

Right: Rival 34, a typical well-appointed cruising boat with a length of 10.36m.

Glossary

Abaft Behind.

Aft The rear part of a vessel.

Alongside Beside, next to.

Amidships The middle part of a vessel.

Anti-fouling Paint applied to discourage marine growths below the waterline.

Astern Behind.

Backstay Stay supporting a mast from aft.

Ballast keel Weighted or heavy keel.

Batten Lath-like length of wood or plastic used to give a sail its correct shape.

Beam A vessel's width at her widest part.

Bearing Direction.

Beat Sail against the wind.

Beaufort Scale Scale of wind speeds.

Bending on Attaching a sail.

Bermudan rig A rig with a triangular mainsail.

Bilge Lowest part of a vessel's hull.

Bilge keels Twin keels fitted one on either side of the centreline of the hull.

Blanket Deprive of wind.

Boom Spar extending the foot of a sail.

Bow The front end of a vessel.

Bowline Type of knot.

Bowsprit Spar extending from the bow to hold out the foot of a sail or sails.

Break out Pull free (an anchor).

Bulkhead Vertical partition separating compartments inside a vessel.

Carvel Hull planking fitted edge-to-edge.

Catamaran Boat with twin hulls.

Catboat Boat with one mast and one sail (*see also* lugsail rig, Una rig).

Centreboard Retractable keel.

Chart Map of an area of water.

Charter Hire.

Cirrus High, wispy cloud.

Class Boats in a particular category.

Cleat Projection round which a rope may be fastened.

Clew Bottom, after corner of a sail.

Clench-built *See* clinker-built.

Chine Angle where two planes of a hull meet.

Clinker-built Method of hull construction in which each plank overlaps the one below it.

Close-hauled Sailing as nearly as possible towards where the wind is coming from.

Cocked hat Small triangle on chart where three position lines cross.

Cringle Eyelet in a sail.

Cockpit Open space where the crew of a cabin boat sit.

Compass card Circular card in the compass bowl.

Compass rose Representation of the compass card on a chart.

Counter Stern.

CQR Plough-type anchor.

Cumulus Cloud formation.

Cutter Vessel with two sails in front of the mast and one behind it.

Dagger board Retractable/removable keel.

Dinghy Small boat propelled by a sail or sails, oars, or an engine.

Doghouse Raised after-part of cabin-top.

Draught Vessel's depth in the water.

Dry out Protrude above the surface as the tide falls.

Ebb tide Falling tide.

Echo-sounder Electronic device for measuring depths.

Fairlead Device for controlling the direction or 'lead' of a rope.

Fender Bumper put over the side to prevent collision damage.

Fetch Distance a vessel will travel on momentum alone.

Figure-of-eight Type of knot.

Fin keel Keel shaped like a fish's fin.

Fisherman's anchor Traditional type of anchor.

Fitting out Getting ready for the sailing season.

Fix Method of determining a vessel's position.

Flare Visual distress signal.

Flashing light A navigational light which flashes at regular intervals.

Flood tide Rising tide.

Fluke Spade-like prong of an anchor.

Foot Bottom edge of a sail.

Fore-and-aft rig Arrangement by which sails can be set from forward to aft.

Foredeck Deck forward of the mast or foremast.

Forepeak Foremost area inside the vessel.

Forestay Stay supporting the mast from the bow.

Formula class Boats with the same performance potential.

Frames Strengthening cross-pieces.

Gaff rig Rig with the mainsail supported by a yard (gaff) at a marked angle to the mast.

Genoa Large foresail.

Glass-fibre Modern synthetic material for boat construction.

Goose-wing Set sails on opposite sides of the boat.

Ground tackle Anchoring equipment.

GRP Glass-fibre reinforced plastic (*see* glass-fibre).

Group flashing Navigational light exhibiting flashes in groups.

Group occulting Navigational light that 'goes out' at regular grouped intervals.

Guard rail Safety wire or wires along the sides of a boat.

Gudgeon Eyelet on the stern on which the rudder pivots (*see also* pintle).

Gunter rig Rig with a short mast and the head of the mainsail supported by an almost perpendicular yard (gaff).

Gybe Altering course down-wind from one tack to the other.

Gymbals Hanging frame for keeping an object level.

Half-ebb Falling tide at the half-way mark.

Halyard Rope used for hoisting a sail.

Hand-bearing compass Compass used for checking the direction of navigational marks.

Handing Lowering a sail or sails.

Hard standing Firm part of beach or waterside which will take the weight of a boat.

Hatch Opening with a 'lid'/doors giving access to the interior of a vessel.

Head Top corner of a sail.

Headroom Height inside a cabin boat.

Headsail Sail in front of the mast.

Heeling Leaning over.

Helm Steering gear.

Helmsman Person steering.

Hitch Simple knot, or part of one.

Hook Popular term for an anchor.

Hull Body of the vessel.

Inboard Within the limits of a vessel.

Inshore Near land.

Jamming cleat Device to prevent a rope running out.

Jib Sail in front of the mast.

Jib-headed rig *See* Bermudan rig.

Keel Backbone of a boat's framework.

Ketch Vessel with two masts, the after one being shorter.

Knock down To be blown over flat on the water.

Lay off (a course) Work out the direction to steer.

Lay up Put a boat away at the end of the sailing season.

Lead and line Weighted rope for measuring depths.

Lee The side of the boat opposite to that on which the wind is blowing.

Lee (by the) Running with the wind on the same side as the mainsail.

Leech After edge of a sail.

Lee helm A boat's tendency to turn away from the wind.

Lee-oh! Helmsman's executive order when tacking.

Lee shore Land on the side of the boat opposite to that on which the wind is blowing.

Leeway Sideways motion.

Legs Posts for supporting a boat on land.

Light air Gentle breeze.

Lightship Moored vessel acting as a navigational aid.

LOA A vessel's maximum length at deck level.

Loose-footed Sail without a boom along the foot.

Lubber line Mark on the compass bowl indicating the boat's fore-and-aft line.

Luff Forward edge of a sail.

Lugsail rig A rig consisting of one mast and one sail (*see also* catboat, Una rig).

LWL Vessel's length on the waterline.

Magnetic north Direction in which the needle of a magnetic compass points.

Mainsail Sail hoisted abaft the mainmast.

Mainsheet Rope controlling the mainsail.

Marconi rig *See* Bermudan rig.

Marina Boat haven, usually with service facilities.

Middle ground Shallow patch in mid-channel.

Mizzen mast After mast of a vessel with more than one mast.

Mizzen sail Sail hoisted on the mizzen mast.

Mono-hull Single-hulled craft.

Mooring Permanent anchor chain or rope, buoyed at the surface.

Moulded hull Hull constructed by bonding thin sheets of wood cross-wise.

Mudberth 'Hole' in the shoreline for mooring a boat.

Multi-hull Boat with more than one hull.

Navel pipe Pipe through which the anchor cable passes from above decks to its stowage below.

Neap tide Tide with minimum rise and fall.

Nimbus Rain cloud.

Occulting light Light which shines most of the time but goes out at regular intervals.

Offshore Away from the land.

One-design Classes of racing craft in which only very minor differences are permitted.

Outboard motor Engine attached to the stern.

Outhaul Rope or line for stretching something taut, most commonly the foot of the mainsail.

Overhangs Differences fore and aft between a boat's LOA and LWL.

Painter Rope attached to a small boat's bows for towing or making fast.

Parallel ruler Device for drawing bearings on a chart.

Pilot A person who steers ships into or out of a harbour, or through difficult water.

Pintle Pin on which a rudder pivots (*see also* gudgeon).

Pipe cot Adjustable, hammock-style berth.

Point (of sailing) Vessel's course relative to the wind.

Port Left-hand side of a vessel looking forward.

Port tack Sailing with the wind on the port side.

Position line Line drawn on a chart when determining a vessel's position.

Pulpit Protective railing round the bows.

Pushpit Protective railing round the stern.

Reach Point of sailing with the wind coming from the side.

Ready about! Helmsman's preparatory order when changing tack.

Reef cringle Eyelet at each end of a row of reef points.

Reefing Reducing sail area.

Reef points Short lengths of line for tying round the surplus part of a sail when reefing.

Restricted class Racing class with particular restrictions as regards hulls and sails.

Retractable keel Keel which can be raised or lowered as required.

Ribs Shaped members attached to the keel at right-angles.

Riding light Light displayed by a vessel at anchor.

Rig Number, shape and arrangement of a vessel's mast(s) and sails.

Roller reefing Reducing sail area by rolling the foot round the boom.

Rudder Vertical board or plate controlling a vessel's course.

Running Sailing with the wind coming from astern.

Running rigging Ropes by which a vessel's sails are hoisted and controlled.

Schooner Sailing vessel with an after mast taller than the forward one.

Scrubbing posts Posts for keeping a boat erect while the bottom is being cleaned.

Set Angle of sails to the wind.

Settee berth Permanent bunk which also serves as seating.

Shackle U-shaped device for attaching a rope to a sail.

Sheave Grooved wheel in a block (pulley).

Sheet Rope used for controlling a sail.

Sheet winch Mechanism for hauling a sheet taut.

Shell The outer casing of a block (*see also* sheave).

Shoal Area of shallow water.

Shroud Stay laterally supporting a mast.

Slack water Period at high and low water when the tide is turning.

Sloop Vessel with one mast and two sails.

Sound signals Sounds made by vessels or navigational marks to indicate their presence.

Spar Pole for supporting or extending a sail.

Spinnaker Light-weather, balloon-type sail.

Spinnaker pole Light spar for extending, the foot of a spinnaker.

Splice Method of joining two ropes.

Spring Mooring rope.

Spring tide Tide with maximum rise and fall.

Stanchion Metal post supporting a guardrail.

Standing rigging Ropes supporting a vessel's mast(s).

Stand on Maintain course and speed.

Starboard The right-hand side looking forward.

Starboard tack Sailing with the wind on the starboard side.

Stay Rope supporting a mast.

Steerage-way Movement through the water.

Stepping Erecting a mast.

Stern The rear end of a vessel.

Stem-post Forward and upwards extension of keel.

Stern-post After and upwards extension of keel.

Storm jib Small, tough jib for very bad weather.

Storm trysail Small, tough sail replacing the mainsail in very bad weather.

Stratus Sheet cloud, usually indicating rain.

Square rig A rig in which the sails are set 'square' across the vessel.

Tack (1) Bottom forward corner of a sail. (2) Course relative to the wind.

Tacking Sailing a zig-zag course against the wind.

Tackle Rope-and-block arrangement, usually for increasing hauling power.

Tail Fibre rope end of a wire halyard.

Taking soundings Checking depths.

Tender Small boat used for getting to and from a larger one.

Tidal range Vertical difference between high and low water.

Tidal stream Current in the sea.

Tide-table 'Calendar' indicating the times of high and low water.

Thimble Metal lining of an eye in a rope.

Tiller Lever by which the rudder is operated.

Topmark Distinguishing mark on the top of a buoy.

Transom Flat stern.

Trim Adjustment of sails to the wind.

Trimaran Boat with three hulls.

Una rig Rig with only one mast and one sail (*see also* lugsail and catboat rig).

Unbend Remove a sail.

Under way Moving under sail or power.

Unlay Separate the strands of a rope.

Unstep Remove (a mast).

Veer Let out (anchor cable).

Warp Rope used for mooring etc.

Weather helm A boat's tendency to turn towards the wind.

Weathering Passing to windward of (usually some mark or other).

Well-found Sound and properly equipped.

Whipping Binding a rope with twine.

Windward The direction the wind is coming from.

Withies Tree branches marking minor channels.

Working rig The sails a vessel normally sets.

Yard Spar used to support or extend a sail.

Yarn Rope fibre.

Yaw Swing from side to side.

Yawl A vessel with two masts, the after one placed far back and very short.

Index

221

Useful Addresses

Dinghy Cruising Association,
33 Blythe Hill Lane,
London SE6 4UP, Britain.

Junior Offshore Group,
149 St. Pancras, Chichester, West
Sussex, Britain.

National Sailing Centre, Arctic
Road, West Cowes, Isle of Wight,
Britain.

**National School Sailing
Association,** Chelstoke,
Lymington Bottom Road,
Medstead, Alton, Hampshire,
Britain.

National Scout Boating Centre,
Longridge, Quarry Wood Road,
Marlow, Buckinghamshire
SL7 2RE, Britain.

Ocean Youth Club,
1 Oak Street, Gosport,
Hampshire PO12 1JN, Britain.

Royal Yachting Association,
Victoria Way, Woking,
Surrey GU21 1EQ, Britain.

Her Majesty's Stationery Office,
Atlantic House, Holborn Viaduct,
London EC1, Britain.

Sail Training Association,
Bosham, Chichester,
Sussex PO18 8HR, Britain.

**International Yacht Racing
Union,** 60 Knightsbridge,
London SW1X 70F, Britain.

Offshore Racing Council,
19 St. James' Place, London SW1,
Britain.

**Australian Yachting
Federation,** 33 Peel Street,
Milson's Point, New South Wales,
Australia 2016.

Canadian Yachting Association
333 River Road (11th Floor),
Vanier, Ottawa KIL 8B9, Ontario
Canada.

**New Zealand Yachting
Federation,** PO Box 4173,
Auckland, New Zealand.

**South African Yacht Racing
Association,** Private Bag 1,
Saxonwold, South Africa.

**United States Yacht Racing
Union,** PO Box 209, Newport,
RI 02840, USA.